WORLD MINERALS
AND
WORLD POLITICS

A FACTUAL STUDY OF MINERALS IN THEIR
POLITICAL AND INTERNATIONAL
RELATIONS

By

C. K. LEITH

KENNIKAT PRESS
Port Washington, N. Y./London

KENNIKAT PRESS SCHOLARLY REPRINTS
Dr. Ralph Adams Brown, Senior Editor

Series on
MAN AND HIS ENVIRONMENT
Under the General Editorial Supervision of
Dr. Roger C. Heppell
Professor of Geography, State University of New York

WORLD MINERALS AND WORLD POLITICS

First published in 1931
Reissued in 1970 by Kennikat Press
Library of Congress Catalog Card No: 74-113286
ISBN 0-8046-1322-2

Manufactured by Taylor Publishing Company   Dallas, Texas

KENNIKAT SERIES ON MAN AND HIS ENVIRONMENT

FOREWORD

NEW mineral problems of a social and political nature, with important bearings on world affairs, are now taking form. The primary cause is a vastly greater consumption of minerals, due to the speeding up of industrial life and its spread through backward nations. Mineral reserves to meet this demand must now be viewed in entirely new perspective. Almost the first effort to take stock of minerals from a world standpoint was made in response to the special and overwhelming mineral demands of the World War, and the investigation has gone on since with ever-widening scope. For the first time in history it is now possible to appraise the world's mineral resources with some approach to accuracy, to anticipate the lineaments of the world mineral geography of the future, and to recognize some of the political implications in the situation.

It appears that certain minerals exist in such large quantities as to give no concern for the future, and that others are definitely limited; that the available resources are not equally distributed among the continents and nations; that no country has really

[v]

adequate amounts of all minerals; that some countries are conspicuously deficient in minerals; that the peaks of production are already passed for some of the most important districts. It appears also that surprisingly few mineral districts really figure largely in meeting modern requirements. Thousands of others which formerly seemed important can be almost disregarded because of their relatively small aggregate contribution to the present requirements.

Countries bordering the North Atlantic, particularly the United States and western Europe. are the fortunate possessors of essential minerals in amounts and combinations necessary for industrial strength. Other parts of the world, notwithstanding popular beliefs to the contrary, are not so fortunate. Their mineral industries must continue to be subordinate or tributary to those of the North Atlantic countries. The thrust of exploitation of world minerals has emanated from the North Atlantic, and will continue to do so. Against this thrust other regions are mainly in a defensive position. Great commercial units of North Atlantic countries, some of them of international scope, have acquired control of vast sections of the mineral industry and have come into conflict with other units similarly engaged. Several minerals have become commercially monopolized and others are well on their way toward this stage.

FOREWORD

World history since the industrial revolution has demonstrated the necessity of industrial power as a basis for political and military supremacy under modern conditions. It now appears that the industrial growth of the North Atlantic countries was not alone a matter of superior enterprise of their peoples, but a response to unusually favorable environmental conditions affording the necessary raw materials, and that there is little promise of similar growth elsewhere because of the fundamental deficiencies in raw materials. The continued political and military preponderance of the North Atlantic region seems to be indicated for the future.

Nations, realizing almost for the first time the vital need of mineral raw materials for their future industrial welfare and safety, have taken active political steps both to secure new supplies and to protect those already in hand from encroachments by outsiders. The problem has become international in scope, not through political intent, but by force of commercial circumstances.

Minerals constitute only a part of what is termed "the natural resource problem," but they furnish a defined basis for an inductive approach to the broader problem. We are just learning to make use of our physical environment; the problem of our mineral resources offers a tempting challenge to our ability to foresee and take intelligent advantage of a new environmental factor, instead, as has been our habit, of allowing ourselves to be overrun by environmental conditions to which we remain passive and more or less oblivious, or to continue on a course which fails to take advantage of the fullest responsibilities.

In the following pages the attempt will be made to outline as simply as possible the principal elements of the new picture, with a view of tracing tendencies and policies in actual operation and pointing out what seem to be the main political problems, national and international, for the future. The dynamic rather than the static aspects will be stressed. The purpose is to present the situation objectively, without expression of personal opinion as to what should or should not be. If, in the interpretation of trends, personal opinion seems to creep in, the author hopes that it will be within limits permissible in a scientific approach to the subject.

C. K. LEITH.

MADISON, WIS.,
December, 1930.

CONTENTS

[ix]

CONTENTS

CHAPTER III

[x]

CONTENTS

CHAPTER IV

CHAPTER V

[xi]

CONTENTS

CHAPTER VI

WORLD MINERALS AND WORLD POLITICS

be, but by the application in the United States of the
provisions of our leasing Act, that foreigners should
be excluded from the development of our public
lands if we were excluded from theirs. Rights have
been conferred on us in exact equality of the use in the
United States and Venezuela of oil. It is often charged
against the United States, and not without . . . . United
States is using the Monroe Doctrine as a cloak to
develop a selfish oil policy. Whether or not the use of
such protest . . . . on the part of the United States
. . . . of the Monroe Doctrine has played any
. . . . . in American interests . . . may be true . . . . . other
. . . . . situations . . . . up misused by foreign
. . . . countries.

The Far East

For parts of the Far East under western political
control the situation has been discussed . . . . in
. . . . connection with the political control of minerals
. . . . . Great Britain, France, Russia, the Netherlands, and the United States. There remain to be
discussed only Japan and China.

Japan.—Japan imposes restrictions which make
it practically impossible for foreign companies to
obtain mining rights in the empire and none such
exist. However, foreign mining companies conduct
operations on a small scale in Korea and Manchuria.
The Japanese government is directly associated in
the operation of some of the mineral resources

Chapter I

NEW ELEMENTS IN THE MINERAL PICTURE

The New Scale of Production

THE quest of iron and copper and flint for use as weapons, and of gold and silver and precious stones for adornment and art, runs far back into history and is associated with many stirring events of exploration and war. But minerals were used on a relatively small scale, even as late as the French Revolution, and constituted only a minor factor in the environmental conditions influencing human activities. With the advent of the industrial revolution of Great Britain, a little more than a century ago, began the real exploitation of earth materials in a way to influence essentially our material civilization. In this short time, at an ever accelerating rate, minerals have become a fundamental basis of industrialism, to be ranked with soil, climate, and other major influences on our activities. Few realize the sweeping range of this change—the fact, for instance, that in a hundred years the output of pig iron, copper, and mineral fuels has increased

[3]

a hundred fold; that more mineral resources have been mined and consumed since the opening of the century than in all preceding history; that in the United States more minerals have been mined and consumed in the last twenty years than in its preceding history; that the per capita consumption of minerals in the United States has multiplied fifteen times in forty years; that the world production of several essential minerals has been doubling about every ten years. The last twenty years have seen as much world gold production as the four hundred years following the discovery of America. A single Lake Superior iron mine now produces every two weeks a volume of ore equivalent to the Great Pyramid of Egypt, which required the toil of vast hordes for several decades and has been long regarded as one of the most stupendous works of man. In 1929 the United States produced more zinc than all of the world did in the first fifty years of the last century. The copper production of the world in 1929 was more than twice as great as the estimated production for all history up to the nineteenth century, and the United States figure for the same year was greater than all the production of the country up to 1888.

By harnessing the power from coal, oil, gas, and water we have multiplied our capacity for work. Energy is being released on a new scale, with consequences which cannot yet be appraised. The production of oil in the United States, for example, is now as great in one year as the aggregate for the first forty years of the industry from the Civil War to the close of the century. As much oil has been consumed in the last eight years, both in the United States and in the world, as in all preceding history. Natural gas consumption in the United States has trebled in the last eight years, and even greater expansion is near at hand. Nor do these figures tell the whole story, for they take no account of the greater efficiency in the use of fuels. As a matter of fact, in the fifteen years from 1913 to 1928 the energy available from mineral fuels and water power in the United States increased 38 per cent while industrial production grew about 70 per cent.

Minerals now constitute about two-thirds of the railway tonnage of the United States and about a quarter of all ocean-borne traffic.

With the advance of industrialism and technology the list of commercial minerals has expanded rapidly in recent years until now it includes over seventy-seven minerals. Few years pass without a use being found for some mineral heretofore regarded as worthless. The aluminum industry is not yet fifty years old and the extensive use of many of the minor minerals dates much more recently.

It is not to be expected that the acceleration of production will continue indefinitely at the present rate. Some substances are not destroyed by use and become available as scrap, the use of which lessens the call on primary ores (see page 34). Technologic processes are making higher recoveries from raw materials, which makes them go farther, as in the case of gasoline from petroleum. Other processes improve the product of manufacture in ways to lower requirements of raw materials. For instance, the rapidly widening use of steel alloys requires less weight of steel and therefore of iron ore. Without these retarding influences, demands for raw materials would in time reach fantastic figures impossible of realization.

The world has just entered on a gigantic experiment in the use of earth materials. In appraising the effect of this new element in human environment there is no historical precedent to guide us, and the change is too recent, too pervasive, for us to understand in all its significance. Yet a few clear tendencies are beginning to be discernible.

Convergence of Demand on the Largest Reserves

Vastly increasing mineral requirements have resulted in the intensive exploitation of the comparatively few mineral reserves capable of meeting these requirements. When the demand was small, it was often possible to secure the necessary supplies from a considerable number of scattered sources. As the mineral industries have grown, the units most favorably situated in regard to raw materials and markets have naturally outstripped the others, thereby deepening and extending the trade channels tributary to them. In each of the principal mineral industries there now stand out a few dominating centers of supply and manufacture. Other regions are handicapped in some essential particulars—in size or grade of reserves, in cost of transportation to markets, or in some other way.

This does not mean that sources of supply are becoming less in number; for some minerals they are actually increasing. Relatively, however, they do not gain in production on the dominant sources.

Iron ores, for example, are widely scattered over the globe, being present in every continent and in almost every country; yet the principal supply is drawn from only a few sources—from the Lake Superior region and Alabama in the United States, from northeastern France and Luxemburg, from the Cleveland, Lincolnshire, Northamptonshire, and Cumberland districts of England, from the Kiruna district of Sweden, and from the Bilbao district of northern Spain. Together, these sources supply about three-fourths of the world's annual total; the remainder comes from scattered sources in many countries.

The steel industries using these iron ores are concentrated in large units, favorably situated where they may draw on the large reserves and where there are adequate supplies of coking coal, together with access to a consuming population.

Of the world's steel-making capacity over 90 per
cent is confined to three regions: the United States,
centering for the most part about the lower Great
Lakes; northeastern England, using both local
ore and coal; and the Ruhr, northeastern France,
and adjacent territories. All of these great units
draw supplementary supplies from outside sources.
As they have become larger and more firmly
entrenched, they have been able to reach farther
afield for the needed raw materials. In no other
region now known would it be possible to duplicate
these large units with equal efficiency. Even if
some location could be found which would apparently satisfy all of the necessary conditions, the
size and efficiency of the units already established,
with their ramifications of allied industry, would
make competition or duplication difficult for the
new unit.

Turning to coal, it appears that the grade of
bituminous coal adapted to coking and to efficient
power uses is most extensively exploited in the
eastern United States, in Great Britain, and in
western Germany, these three regions producing
about two-thirds of the world's supply. The remaining third comes from many sources, no one
of which is in a class with the sources named. The
United States has about half of the world's estimated reserves. All the countries of the southern
hemisphere have together less than one-tenth of

the estimated reserves. In China there are large reserves of proper grade for commercial use, but they are not used because of the lack of industrial development and initiative on the part of the Chinese.

The anthracite production of the world is still more concentrated, being confined practically to eastern Pennsylvania. Over 95 per cent of the world's total comes from that region, the remainder coming mainly from Wales. The only large reserves in sight are the yet unexploited reserves of China.

In the last five years the United States has produced 69 per cent of the world's supply of petroleum; Russia, Mexico, Venezuela, Persia, the Dutch East Indies, and Colombia (named in the order of their production) have accounted for 24 per cent, while the remaining 7 per cent has been scattered among other countries, each of which produced less than 1 per cent. Of the oil produced in the United States 50 per cent comes from 2 per cent of the producing wells. About 85 per cent of the world's refining capacity is concentrated in the United States. The location of the great oil reserves of the future is not nearly so well known as is the case with other mineral commodities, and important shifts in the geography of the industry are to be expected. If one makes large allowance for such shifts, however, it seems clear that in the future, as in the past, the oil industry will be dominated by a very few districts.

The United States produces nearly 55 per cent of the world's copper, and of this nearly 90 per cent comes from a few mines in Utah, Arizona, Montana, Michigan, and Alaska. Another 18 per cent of the world's production comes from Chile and Peru. Additional large sources for the future will be Rhodesia, the Congo, and Ontario. The companies controlling the major production of the world are even fewer in number than the principal mines.

The minerals known as the ferro-alloys, necessary in the making of iron and steel, are derived from a very few principal sources. Manganese ore comes mainly from limited districts in India, Georgia (southern Russia), Gold Coast (Africa), and Brazil; chromite comes from Rhodesia, India, and New Caledonia; nickel for the most part comes from a single district in Canada; tungsten comes from China (50 per cent of the total); and about half of the world's vanadium comes from Peru.

The Malay States, Bolivia, and Dutch East Indies account for 85 per cent of the world's tin production. The Union of South Africa produces over half of the world's gold (principally from the Transvaal district) and over two-thirds of the total comes from the British Empire. The Transvaal has produced gold to the value of over five billions of dollars. Mexico and the United States account for two-thirds of the world's silver production, mainly from half a dozen districts. The United States is the greatest lead-producing country, yielding about 40 per cent of the world's output; Mexico, Australia, and Spain yield about 30 per cent. As for zinc, the United States in 1928 produced about 40 per cent of the world's output, and 70 per cent of it came from three districts.

The potash deposits of the Stassfurt district of Germany and, secondarily, those in Alsace, dominate the world's markets. Natural nitrates, used in peace times for fertilizers, come almost solely from Chile. The sulphur markets of the world are monopolized by the production from Texas, with minor participation of Sicily.

These illustrations are perhaps sufficient to establish the fact that the dominating centers of mineral production are few. About thirty of the principal mineral districts account for over three-fourths of the value of the world's mineral production. In any picture of the world mineral situation, then, there stand out a few nodal points, pretty well fixed for the future, with ramifications usually extending far beyond national boundaries and crossing one another in the most intricate fashion.

Interdependence of Nations

An obvious consequence of concentration of mineral production is that nations are mutually interdependent in regard to mineral supplies. Even the most favored nation must look outside of its boundaries for essential minerals, and many nations lack almost all of the necessary minerals.

If the situation is viewed in another way, there is a growing tendency toward specialization in minerals among the nations. The United States, for instance, has led the world in production of oil and copper, and great industrial combinations have been built up. Experience, organization, money, and technical skill thereby mobilized are projected into copper and oil districts in all parts of the world, with the result that the United States has become the world purveyor for these commodities. In a similar way Great Britain has dominated the tin industry and Germany the potash industry. Competition by other nations becomes increasingly difficult, because nowhere else is there the same combination of raw materials and organization to do the job as efficiently.

This situation is partly new, because of the new scale. It raises new political questions of an unprecedented nature, which bear on the future orderly development and peace of the world.

International Flow of Minerals

It follows also from the concentration of mineral production in a few regions that the principal mineral trade routes must necessarily be few in number and cross national boundaries. A substantial portion of the minerals produced is consumed outside the countries of origin. In fact, nearly a third of the world's mineral tonnage moves across international boundaries (of this third, coal, oil, and iron constitute the great mass).

The necessity of world-wide movements of minerals puts a premium on freedom of the seas in peace and control of the seas in war. The key to the problem is to be found mainly in the convergence of mineral trade routes of the north Atlantic Ocean. The interruption of any one of the main channels of movement between nations is followed by confusion or disaster, because of the difficulty, sometimes the impossibility, of making up the supply of minerals from other sources. This was strikingly manifested in the Great War. Failure to comprehend this simple fact underlies many futile attempts to close or change these routes by political action.

Concentration of Commercial and Political Control of Minerals

Mineral deposits large enough to count in the present world picture are coming under fewer and larger units of commercial control at a rate which is still accelerating. For some minerals there is already an approach to world monopoly by single companies or cooperating groups of companies, as illustrated by nickel, vanadium, aluminum, potash, asbestos, mercury, diamonds, bismuth, sulphur, and natural nitrates. For others the control is more divided, though still in sufficiently few hands to make world cooperation potentially possible. In this category may be mentioned copper, iron, lead, oil, tin, and manganese. Two companies control 34 per cent of the world's copper production. Five oil companies produce 35 per cent of the world's petroleum. National cartels are numerous in all the industrial countries of Europe. International combinations which can be classed as cartels have been formed for raw steel, zinc, copper, pig iron, ferromanganese, diamonds, magnesia, nitrogenous fertilizers, and many other commodities. For still others the supplies are so widely scattered and abundant that ownership is likewise widely distributed, as in coal, zinc, clays, and building stones. The fact that the movement toward monopoly control has gone much farther for some minerals than for others is due for the most part to physical conditions inherent in the industries themselves, such, for instance, as size and geographic distribution of the principal reserves. But there is also clearly discernible the influence of strong leadership in some mineral industries which has not yet come to the front in others. Whether the movement is advanced or just starting, it is almost without exception in the same direction for all minerals.

Thus far the commercial control of minerals is lodged first in the commercial organizations of the United States, second in those of Great Britain. Fully three-quarters of the world's mineral production and reserves are controlled from these sources. Competition for further control is now on between these two. Commercial units of other countries have been hopelessly outdistanced, but are still striving.

Commercial control takes varied aspects. It may consist of ownership of the mineral reserves, or it may be exercised indirectly through ownership of smelters, refineries, pipe lines, and transportation lines, or through selling agencies, cartels, or associations of one kind or another. A common form of control is the so-called vertical trust. Nearly all of the iron ore, for instance, is owned and operated by manufacturers of iron and steel, and bauxite is owned by manufacturers of aluminum. Copper-mining companies have added manufacturing outlets by the acquisition of brass companies.

The integration of the mineral industry has been for the most part within the industrial fields of the individual minerals, but to a less extent there is a noticeable tendency for the extension of unit operation over several minerals. This is particularly true of industries which carry their products through to finished manufactures, such as the iron and steel business, which controls not only iron ores but

[15]

considerable amounts of coal, limestone, zinc, and the ferro-alloy minerals. Copper companies manufacturing brass also control notable zinc supplies needed for brass or bronze. In still other cases the mixture of minerals in large ore bodies brings a variety of minerals under one ownership. The smelting control of complex ores leads to the same result.

When through a fortunate combination of raw materials, demand, competent management, and adequate capital, a thriving mineral industry develops, it is likely to become the center of an ever-widening sphere of commercial influence reaching farther and farther afield for new supplies, and eventually transcending national boundaries. In time its sphere impinges on that of other growing units, with the not uncommon sequence of intensified competition, cooperation, and, finally, merger. Unification has usually brought conservational advances in production, manufacturing, and distribution. The growth of a large unit puts smaller scattered competitors in such a disadvantageous position that they are more or less compelled to combine as a defensive measure. Concentration of commercial control has already tied up so much of the world's mineral resources that the possibilities for acquirement of reserves by new purchasers are very limited. On the other hand, there is a growing surplus of current production for most minerals.

One of the purposes of commercial unification is the more intelligent handling of this surplus.

The international spread of unit control has been hindered and deflected by various political measures designed to foster domestic industries. Tariffs and taxes (see pages 102–105) have been freely used as defensive measures against outside commercial control. When the barriers thus set up become too high, the controlling unit operating from without often finds it necessary to form separate companies and to build up local mining, smelting, or manufacturing to a greater extent than might be necessary or desirable if the political barriers did not exist. Nevertheless, there is a steady trend toward common ownership and centralized direction of the industry.

As minerals have come under fewer and larger commercial units there has likewise been a concentration of political control. A large part of the earth's minerals has come under the political influence of the British Empire and the United States. Even where minerals are in widely scattered commercial units, they may have a common background of political affiliation, as in the case of the world's gold, 70 per cent of which is owned commercially by British interests, or the world's copper which is dominated by American interests. More direct and centralized controls are those of nitrate by Chile, potash by Germany and France, tin by

[17]

Great Britain, nickel by Canada, mercury by Spain and Italy, and others.

The problem as to who shall ultimately own the world's minerals now looms before a rather startled world. While the problem has been slowly shaping itself for some time, it is only with the newly gained perspective of the limited distribution of the sources capable of supplying the new demands, and of the fact that monopolistic controls of these sources are rapidly eventuating, that the problem begins to emerge into public consciousness as one of real national and international concern. What political unit or combination or method shall control the commercial organizations of world scope? It is only this question which is now delaying some of the larger steps in commercial integration. This question is discussed in another chapter.

To some extent commercial and political integration is under way also in other raw materials like rubber, coffee, and other special crops, but there is a fundamental difference. Minerals are irreplaceable assets, more scantily and erratically localized about the globe than the necessary environmental conditions for the growth of special crops. They are less susceptible to expansion by human effort, and have present and potential scarcity or monopoly values not inherent in anything the soil produces.

NEW ELEMENTS IN THE PICTURE

Exploitation

Another clear consequence of vast demand is the necessity for finding and developing adequate sources of mineral supply wherever they may be found. This effort naturally originates in countries with prosperous mineral industries and does not stop with national boundaries. It is but natural that our oil, copper, iron, aluminum, and other mineral industries should be leaders in exploitation of these minerals abroad. Foreign exploitation becomes a more and more conspicuous element in the mineral picture. Large known or potential mineral reserves exist in many countries without the capital, initiative, or skill necessary for development. Exploitation by foreign capital is necessary to make such minerals available to the world. Usually this aid is welcomed, but if not, exploitation goes on by commercial and political compulsion. Whether right or wrong, demand is apparently beyond public control. As long as we individually demand automobiles and other mechanical conveniences, we are creating a mandate to secure raw materials obtainable only beyond our national borders.

The primary meaning of the word "exploit" is to develop, or get the value out of, but there has come to be attached to it the idea of unfairness, selfishness, and force which is now reflected in supplementary definitions in dictionaries. In the public mind the objectionable connotations so overshadow the primary meaning that the term has come to stand for one of the most objectionable of human activities. The term is here used mainly in its primary sense, but not exclusively so. If a less provocative term like "develop" were substituted, it would probably not be understood by most people as covering essentially the same activity which has come historically to be known as exploitation. A term is needed which will identify the facts, whether they are regarded as good or bad. Even the best of *development* is seldom completely free from selfishness and unfairness; the worst of *exploitation* is seldom without some underlying justification in world needs.

The history of exploitation shows that our own and other governments have almost never frankly disclosed the exploitation being done by their nationals. They are keen to "protect legitimate interests" of their nationals, but deplore or ignore "exploitation." On the other hand, opponents of imperialistic tendencies are likely to condemn all exploitation as pernicious, without recognition of its essential need. Exploitation of necessary resources is no more right or wrong than was nature's distribution of resources. One of the keenest philosophic writers on foreign affairs, Captain Mahan,[1]

[1] MAHAN, A. T., "Problem of Asia," p. 98, Little, Brown & Company, 1900.

has perhaps done as well as anybody in claiming this course as a natural right:

The claim of an indigenous population to retain indefinitely control of territory depends not upon a natural right, but upon political fitness . . . shown in the political work of governing, administering and developing, in such manner as to insure the natural right of the world at large that resources should not be left idle but be utilized for the general good. Failure to do this justifies in principle, compulsion from outside; the position to be demonstrated, in the particular instance, is that the necessary time and the fitting opportunity have arrived.

Without exploitation our land would still be in the hands of the aborigines. Has the world benefited as a whole by the change? We hope it is for the good of the greatest number, and can make out a good case for this point of view, when all the elements of exploitation are taken into account; but we cannot prove it.

Foreign exploitation of minerals is, then, an inevitable consequence of the highly irregular distribution of mineral reserves among the nations. The manner of exploitation may be controlled or modified, but the necessity of exploitation cannot be eliminated. To dismiss it as unethical, or undesirable, or unnecessary, as if it were a mere matter of political will, as is sometimes attempted, merely postpones the time when it must be objectively studied and intelligently controlled.

[21]

Chapter II

THE FUTURE GEOGRAPHY OF MINERAL SOURCES

THE history of mineral production has shown many shifts in geographic distribution, due to exhaustion, discovery of new fields, technological advances, substitution and new uses, and various political and commercial influences. This fact is often cited as a reason why it is unsafe to draw political inferences from the present situation. Our thesis is that geographic changes will continue, but that the major shifts for the next few decades are pretty well anticipated and planned for by the mineral industry. Many of the great shifts of the past have been slow and cumulative, however sudden and spectacular they seem when foreshortened in historical perspective, and this is likely to hold true to a much larger extent in the future. The mineral industry presents a moving and not a still picture, but the various possibilities of change have been sufficiently explored to warrant the belief that the geographic distribution of mineral sources is predictable on broad lines for the future. Reasons for this belief are set forth in following pages.

[22]

Changes of Geography Due to Exhaustion of Mineral Deposits

Hundreds of mineral deposits have been exhausted in all parts of the world and many more are on the decline, with increasing costs of extraction. Especially notable is the passing of the older mineral districts in Europe. Among these are most districts yielding copper, lead, iron, and tin in Great Britain, iron and lead in Spain, and silver in Germany. An interesting study of the rise and decline of metal production in various parts of Europe has been made by Hewett who points out that the cycle ordinarily includes five stages shown by successive culminations of (1) the quantity of exports of crude ore, (2) the number of mines in operation, (3) the number of smelters or refining units in operation, (4) the production of metal from domestic ore, and (5) the quantity of imports of crude ore.[1] Other outstanding cases are the decline of the gold and silver production of Australia, and the oil production of Mexico.

In the United States the most notable declines have been in gold and silver mines, including Comstock, Goldfield, Tonopah, Leadville, Aspen, Cripple Creek, California and Alaska placer deposits, and many more. The peak of the United States gold production was reached in 1915. The

[1] HEWETT, D. F., Cycles in Metal Production, *Technical Publication* 183, Am. Inst. Mining Met. Eng., p. 26, March, 1929.

[23]

peak of the oil production from the Appalachians was reached in 1900. The zinc deposits of the Tri-state district of the Mississippi valley are now on the decline, and will be a lesser source of metal in another ten years. Production of iron ores from the Lake Superior region is approaching the maximum and will be well on the decline in the next twenty years. Twelve districts have produced 90 per cent of the copper of the United States. At least six of these have passed their zenith, including the Keweenaw district of Michigan and the Butte district of Montana. While the United States production is still rising, its percentage to the rest of the world is falling.

The shift from an old district to a new usually begins long before ore reserves are actually exhausted, because it is usually impossible to maintain a full rate of output for the last of the reserves. Costs may increase for this reason and because of increasingly adverse conditions, particularly great depth. Where the reserves are known to be limited, also, this may affect plans for new plant construction, causing it to be transferred to places determined by sources of the longest-lived supply rather than in old locations, as illustrated by the present consideration of the advisability of new blast-furnace construction about the Great Lakes based on Lake Superior iron ore, which is known to have a definitely limited life.

Considered broadly, exhaustion of lower grade reserves is still very far in the future, but the world is rapidly passing out of the stage of exploitation of its richest and most accessible mineral deposits into a stage of production based on lower grade deposits of far longer life. In this stage geographic shifts will be fewer, slower, and more easily and certainly anticipated.

Discovery of New Mineral Districts

Heretofore, discovery of new reserves has about kept pace with increasing consumption. For some minerals and for some districts reserves have relatively increased; for others reserves have lessened. Past success in finding new reserves and consideration of the vast amount of ground yet to be explored, in area and in depth, create a strong presumption that discovery will continue for a considerable time to keep up with increased consumption. On the other hand, the period of intensive use of minerals has been short, augmentation of demand has been fast and large, and shortages are beginning to loom here and there which are not being compensated by discovery. The rate of discovery is distinctly lessening.

Gold has a wider appeal to prospectors than almost any other mineral, and the search for it has not been confined to particular times or places or people. Yet there has not been a single maj discovery of gold in the United States for twenty-five years. The last were Goldfield and Tonopah. Notwithstanding steady demand, and discoveries in the Porcupine and Kirkland Lake districts of Canada and elsewhere, the peak of world production was passed in 1915. The last outstanding lead discovery in the United States was the Coeur d'Alene district of Idaho in 1886. Major copper discoveries within the boundaries of the United States since the development of the low-grade porphyry coppers in the southwest between 1900 and 1910 have been confined to extensions of old districts, principally in Arizona, with the addition of the Ajo district of Arizona and one or two of less consequence. No great iron ore discovery has been made in the United States since the opening of the Lake Superior ranges. Unceasing efforts have been made to find tin outside of the great sources of Malay, Dutch East Indies, Siam, Bolivia, and Nigeria. Hundreds of localities containing the proper geologic conditions have been carefully investigated, and special bonuses have been offered by governments, without success. Except for oil, a major source of minerals has not been discovered in Europe since 1850, in the United States since 1910. The important discoveries since 1910 lie in central Africa, Canada, South America, and Australia. Doubtless the future holds promise in Africa, Australia, and Asia.

Discovery of new mineral districts will undoubtedly continue to modify many features of the present geography of mineral production, but some of the geographic trends of discovery are fixed by known geologic conditions. With the present scale of demand only the very large reserves count. In outlying parts of the world, particularly, they must be large enough to warrant large expenditures for development and transportation. Many thousands of small deposits remain to be found in unexpected places, many where heavy vegetation has heretofore prevented systematic prospecting, but most specialists are skeptical about finding major supplies outside of certain favorable geologic formations, the distribution of which is now generally known. For instance, there is no use in hunting for oil in areas of igneous, metamorphic, or pre-Cambrian rocks, which occupy such a large part of the earth's surface. Oil has never been found there in quantity, and there is good reason to believe that it never will be. Certain other geologic conditions are known to be favorable for oil occurrence. Such conditions can now be pretty well traced around the earth, and the general trend of future discoveries indicated. A considerable share of the oil produced in the next ten years will come from deeper horizons in fields that are already producing. The greatest reserves of high-grade iron ore have shown a remarkable tendency to occur in the late pre-Cambrian terranes in the United States, Brazil, India, and South Africa. The distribution of the pre-Cambrian is fairly well known and, therefore, the limiting possibilities of geographic extension of this class of deposits. High-grade coals are definitely limited in their stratigraphic occurrence, and the position and extent of the favorable horizons are now approximately mapped the world over. The general direction of the future shift in copper production is foreshadowed. Copper developments now under way in Chile, Peru, Rhodesia, the Congo, and Canada will take care of the future for a long time.

In response to augmented commercial demand the resources of modern science, transportation, and finance have been brought to bear on the problem of finding new supplies on a scale never before dreamed of. Beginning with airplane reconnaissance and photography, following through to the application of a vast array of new geophysical methods of exploration, and finally by drilling and underground work with modern machinery, all backed by ample capital able to command the best expert service, as much is now done in one year as was done in many years before the opening of the century. In the face of this concerted attack, the steady dwindling of results can but bring conviction that we are approaching the limit of discovery of major mineral areas. Technology, on the other hand, is opening new vistas.

Geographic Changes Due to Technology

While the curve of geographic discovery is flattening, the curve of technologic advances is rapidly rising. It begins to appear that the great discoveries of the future will in the main relate to recovery and use of minerals. Technology has shown the way to use large low-grade copper supplies. It will doubtless do the same for iron ore and aluminum, but much more slowly, owing to the vast extent of rich ores concentrated by nature. Our available reserves of coal and oil have been vastly increased by better methods of extraction and utilization. Such changes will modify the mineral geography of the future, but the locations of these changes are already known in large part. In the hunt for high-grade supplies of minerals the large low-grade sources have also become known, and, therefore, the most likely points of attack for the new technology.

Great successes of technology in recent years, especially in chemistry, have led to the assertion by certain technologists that future successes of the same kind would completely change the picture, that synthesis might even make industry largely independent of the present sources of mineral supply. One must be hopeful, indeed, if he expects

[29]

to synthesize substitutes on the stupendous scale of nature's laboratories, and only such a scale will meet present and future demands. Scale and cost are the considerations that eliminate many commercial applications of successful laboratory experiments. The geographic influences of past technologic changes, viewing the mineral industry as a whole, have shifted the emphasis toward reserves of lower grade and materially lessened the demand for primary ores, but have not sprung the limits of production beyond fields definitely determined by geologic conditions.

Geographic Changes Caused by Substitution

Closely related to technology is the question of substitution. A common bugaboo in parts of the mineral industry is the possibility that substitution of one mineral for another will result in sweeping changes in the relative use of minerals, and therefore in the commercial and geographic distribution of the industry. A review of a long list of partial substitutions which have been made indicates that they have had modifying effects on relative demand for minerals and on price, but have not essentially and permanently changed the world mineral picture. As the field of one mineral is invaded by another, ground is often recovered by finding new uses, or invading other mineral fields.

[30]

In some cases the general public attaches a distorted importance to substitutions because of a lack of knowledge of the materials involved. Interest was aroused when a large automobile manufacturer substituted stainless steel for plated brass in the exposed metal parts of the car. An analysis shows that this steel contains considerable proportions of chromium and nickel, which were previously the chief plating materials, and that more copper is used in the car as a whole than before.

One of the most generally known and widely discussed substitutions is that of oil, gas, and water power for coal as an energy source. Coal production reached its peak in the United States in 1918, when its contribution was 85 per cent of the total energy units from coal, oil, gas, and water power. Ten years later its contribution had fallen to 67 per cent. Total energy utilized has risen at a steady rate, but the rate of coal production has failed to rise proportionally because of the expanding use of energy from other sources.[1] This has been a factor in the overproduction from coal fields which had adapted their operations to the rising curve of the past, and in the social problems consequent thereon, but it has had very little

[1] See HAMMOND, JOHN HAYES, and F. G. TRYON, National Supplies of Power, *Proc.* Intern. Conf. Bituminous Coal, pp. 192–209, 1926; also TRYON, F. G., An Index of Consumption of Fuels and Water Power, *Jour. Am. Stat. Assoc.*, pp. 271–282, September, 1927.

effect on the major geographic distribution of the coal industry. Some of this substitution has been uneconomic, and the oil supply available for the future does not promise that substitution for coal can go much farther. Our relatively limited supply of oil is likely to be more valuable for other purposes for which coal cannot be utilized. In fact it appears that ultimately, upon the depletion of oil reserves, the world may return to coal, some of which may be transformed to an oil by hydrogenation, as a source of energy.

The use of natural gas, now contributing 8 per cent of energy requirements, is on the increase, but at most it will supplement and not become an essential substitute for coal. Water power contributes only about 7 per cent of the total supply of energy, equivalent to about 64,000,000 tons of coal, and further substitution is indicated for the future, but in view of the probable future increase of total energy requirements, and the commercial limitations on harnessing all known sources of water power, it appears likely that water power will remain as a minor source of energy as compared with coal.

Successful experiments in the production of oil from the hydrogenation of coal have tended to create a popular belief that we are about to be relieved from our dependence on natural oil, but the oil industry views this process only as one which will supplement natural sources in the future when higher prices make it commercially feasible. To produce oil on the present scale by the hydrogenation of coal would mean increasing coal production by about 50 per cent and would involve immense capital investment. Also the oil-shale resources of the United States could supply the domestic demands for oil for many years, but a mining industry, with a production one and one-half times as great as the coal-mining industry, would have to be developed in order to meet the present rate of consumption. Oil will continue to come from natural sources until scarcity forces reliance on higher cost alternatives. Even when this time comes, the direction of geographic shift is limited to the known coal and oil-shale reserves.

Aluminum may be produced from common clay in the laboratory but at such cost that the process will almost certainly be postponed until the world's bauxite deposits approach exhaustion. Advantage will be taken as long as possible of the work which nature has done in making such substances, even though we can duplicate the process in the laboratory.

The substitution of aluminum for tin plating or galvanizing or iron alloys for copper has been regarded as something of a threat to the copper industry, but experience has thus far shown that there is plenty of room for all in their own special fields, and the area of overlapping is not great or vital to the prosperity of these industries.

The growing use of scrap of some metals has been viewed with apprehension by the mining industry as possibly a deterrent to future production of primary ores, thereby minimizing the importance of present sources of supply. Copper scrap, for instance, has been called the largest copper mine in the world. Methods for the recovery of scrap metals are rapidly developing. As long as consumption expands, the use of scrap is likely only to retard the rate of primary metal production, not reverse it. With stable or decreasing consumption, this factor will in time result in actual decrease of primary production. In either case the geography of primary production will be determined, as now, by the distribution of the largest, best, and most available reserves.

Geographic Changes Due to Governmental Influence

There remain to be considered geographic shifts caused primarily or greatly accelerated by government action in the form of financial or political aid, bounties, tariffs, embargoes, or other measures. This factor is the most difficult to isolate and measure, and it involves a wide range of factors discussed in subsequent chapters. It will suffice here to say merely that thus far it has only slightly modified the distribution of production, that in the future its influence may be more marked, but not to the extent of changing the principal lines in the picture drawn by nature.

Illustrative Changes Due to Causes Previously Named

Some of the outstanding changes now under way or clearly discerned for the future, due to some combination of the factors above named, may be briefly indicated.

Oil and Gas.—As the oil fields of Pennsylvania and West Virginia have failed in their production, the center of gravity of the industry has shifted to the southwestern United States and California, a change which has been going on for thirty years. While scattering discoveries have been made and will be made outside of these fields, there exist nowhere else in the United States geologic conditions which promise any major shift from the present great sources. The large production of oil from Mexico came from surprisingly few wells, draining great areas of cavernous limestone. The rise of the Mexican field was spectacular; its fall was equally so. Political conditions have hampered exploitation. The chance for repetition of its large production is small, but if it comes it is likely to be in a short-lived spurt of the same spectacular character. The output from Venezuela and adjacent parts of South America has rapidly risen in recent years and will doubtless continue to do so for some time in the future.

[35]

In the farther future the entire strip of territory on
the east slope of the Andes throughout South
America seems likely to yield large quantities of oil
as they are needed and made accessible by development of transportation. Geologists are all agreed
that the great oil-producing area extending from
Rumania in southern Europe eastward beyond the
Black and Caspian seas into Persia and Mesopotamia (Iraq) is potentially most promising for
future development. The curve of production from
this general source will almost surely rise for a long
time to come. The production from the Dutch
East Indies is likely to increase, but it seems to be
the consensus of expert opinion that this will not
materially change the relative contribution of the
East Indies to world demands. Sakhalin Island and
eastern Siberia may show developments, though
the results of work already done have been somewhat disappointing. Much has been hoped of
Africa but a large amount of geologic work done in
recent years has disclosed conditions which materially dampen the hope that this continent will ever
figure very largely in the world oil perspective.[1]

The United States produces about 98 per cent of
the world's natural gas. Formerly this came mainly

[1] For a general summary of the petroleum resources of foreign
countries see "Petroleum Resources of Foreign Countries and Outlying
Possessions of the United States," by A. H. Redfield. *Report* III of
the Federal Oil Conservation Board to the President of the United
States, Appendix C, pp. 50–191, Feb. 25, 1929.

from the Appalachian fields, but the center of production for the future will be Oklahoma, Kansas, Texas, and Louisiana. Canada is the only foreign country which seems to hold much promise for a large-scale production of natural gas. There has been some utilization of gas in Russia, Mexico, Poland, and Rumania, but on a rather small scale, and the rest of the world appears to have poor prospects for any wide expansion of gas production.

Coal.—The principal changes under way in coal production in the United States are the lessening of anthracite production in favor of bituminous production, the slowing up of combined total production because of substitution of oil, gas, and water power as sources of energy, and the small and slow beginnings of a larger use of lignite and semibituminous coal in the western United States. In Canada there is a growing movement of coal from Alberta and the Maritime Provinces toward the principal consuming centers in Ontario, thereby lessening importation of American coal. This shift is being brought about by improvement of transportation and of methods of mining and utilization, under strong pressure and aid from the Dominion and Provincial governments. In Great Britain there are local shifts in the centers of production, owing to increasing costs, arising from increased depth and other adverse physical conditions. The great change on the continent is the remarkable advance in the

[37]

production of lignite by Germany, made possible by the application of new methods of utilization and the large use of by-products, and accelerated by government aid. The loss of the Silesian coal fields was an important cause of this great effort to make Germany self-sustaining. In the distant future we may expect a large growth in production of coal from northeastern China, the world's largest undeveloped reserve of high-grade coal. Minor increases may be looked for in New South Wales, South Africa, and India.

Iron Ore.[1] —The geography of iron ore production will be slowly modified owing to increasing consumption and the exhaustion of such outstanding supplies as those of Spain and, at a considerably later date, those of the Lake Superior region. Larger production may be expected from the great reserves of the southeastern United States and Newfoundland, and possibly also from England. Brazilian iron ores will be used by Europe and the United States. There will be greater importations by Europe from North Africa, and by the United States from Cuba. Iron and steel production in the United States is likely to show some migration to the Atlantic coast, reflecting the growing dependence on foreign iron ore supplies. India, South Africa, Russia, and Australia are likely to increase their production

[1] LEITH, C. K., "The World's Iron Ore Supply," paper read at the World Engineering Congress, Tokio, Japan, November, 1929.

[38]

mainly for local uses. India with the largest high-grade reserves on the Pacific basin may become a considerable exporter of ore. The Far East will show little increase, except possibly in the Philippines and the Dutch East Indies in the more distant future.

There are possibilities of further discoveries of large iron ore deposits principally in the remote regions of the world. Probably even such deposits would become tributary to the centers already established, but if they should prove eventually to be adequate for large development, it is practically certain that many years must elapse before their influence upon the geography of the iron and steel industry begins to be largely felt.

Beneficiation of low-grade iron ore promises no great geographic changes. Its largest application in the United States, for instance, undoubtedly will be in the Lake Superior region, the present center of ore production.

Copper.—The obvious trends in copper are the falling off of Lake Superior and Butte production due to diminishing reserves and higher costs, relative increase in production for the southwest, particularly for low-grade porphyry and disseminated deposits, a decrease in the future percentage of United States production to the world's total, increase from the Andean region of South America from developments already well under way, and the growing relative importance of the coppers of Canada and of the Congo and Rhodesia in Africa. The spectacular advances in technology which made possible the use of the low-grade copper and disseminated ores are not likely to be repeated by similar radical changes. The locus for the further application of these processes is already pretty well indicated.

Zinc.—Notable changes in the geographic distribution of zinc production are now under way. The Tri-state district of the Mississippi valley has about reached its peak and is already drawing on its lower-grade supplies. New Jersey production will lessen, also owing to exhaustion. Eastern Tennessee is on the upgrade. The perfection of flotation processes and introduction of electrolytic smelting are making available large quantities of zinc from the western United States, considerable parts of which could not formerly be recovered at a profit. The result is a gradual increase of production in Utah, Montana, Idaho, and other western states. The production of Canada is increasing from the great Sullivan Mine of British Columbia and will increase greatly from large reserves found in Manitoba, in the Sudbury nickel district, and in Quebec. Newfoundland also has an important new discovery. Mexico has potentially larger production, owing both to discovery and to recovery of zinc from complex ores by the flotation process. In Europe the Spanish production is on the downgrade. New processes have stimulated the production of zinc from Italy. The Broken Hill district of Australia, which has before been the largest producer in the world, shows lessening production, while the Bawdwin district of Burma is still on the upgrade. Looked at broadly, it appears that the United States and Australia percentages of world production are likely to lessen in the future; Canada, Mexico, and South America to rise, and Europe about to hold its own.

Lead.—With the exception of Mount Isa, Australia, and the Sullivan Mine, British Columbia, no really large new sources of lead have been developed during the present century. The production of lead from Europe has been steadily falling off, and the output has increased from the United States, Canada, Mexico, and Burma, principally Mexico and Canada. Further changes in these directions seem likely. Large reserves of low-grade ore are known to be available, when cost warrants their use.

Ferro-alloy Minerals.—In the entire group of ferro-alloy minerals, that is, accessory minerals needed in the manufacture of iron and steel, no revolutionary geographic changes are in sight. This list includes manganese, tungsten, vanadium, nickel, fluorite, zirconium, titanium, chromium, and others. Changing technology, commercial expediency, and governmental influence will here and there cause geographic shifts of production, but the main sources for the future seem to be definitely in sight.

Potash.—The reserves near Stassfurt in Germany and Alsace in France are sufficient to supply the world for an indefinitely long period, and will undoubtedly continue to dominate the future potash industry of the world, but deposits are known in various outlying regions which may in the future figure more largely. These are in Poland, the United States, Russia, Spain, Ethiopia, and the brines of the Dead Sea of Palestine.

The potash deposits of the United States are capable of further large development, particularly in the Permian basin of Texas and adjacent states, and the Searles Lake deposits of California, but high prices caused by import tariffs or war conditions will be necessary to obtain this.

Bauxite.—The aluminum industry is likely to draw more largely in the future on the bauxite deposits widely distributed through the equatorial regions. In anticipation of the larger use of foreign supplies the Aluminium, Limited (under the same stock ownership as the Aluminum Company of America) is developing a large reduction plant in the lower St. Lawrence valley based on water power. This is an outstanding example of a shift in the locus of manufacturing to a source of power so located as to allow access to distant parts of the world.

Graphite.—A comparison of the production of graphite since the war with the pre-war figures reveals the fact that Ceylon is declining and Madagascar is rising and the other countries have maintained a rather even pace. Much of the decline of Ceylon is due to the competition of cheaper graphite from Madagascar, some of it may be attributed to the approaching exhaustion of the deposits, and some to the falling off in the manufacture of graphite crucibles, which absorbed a large part of the Ceylonese production.

Gold.[1]—While no major changes are anticipated in the ranking of the gold-producing districts of the world, the Rand, now accounting for about one-half of the world output, is soon expected to decline. Declines have already been noted in Australia and the United States and a larger proportion of the future gold in the United States will doubtless come from smelters that treat base-metal ores. The world production has been falling off since 1915 and upon the approaching exhaustion of the Rand, there may be a serious shortage. Gold discoveries of magnitude are becoming rare, those in the Porcupine and Kirkland Lake districts of Canada being the only ones in North America in the last twenty-five years. Because of its intimate relation to finance, the problem of the gold supply is of special concern (see page 162).

[1] See Interim Report of the Gold Delegation of the Financial Committee, League of Nations Documents, 1930, II, 26.

Summary of Geographic Changes

If due allowance is made, then, for discovery of new mineral districts, for changes in geography dependent upon technologic advances, and for substitution, it appears that for some minerals, such as tin and gold, there is little prospect for major geographic changes for a very long time. For other minerals, including coal, iron, and copper, slow changes are now under way, but the geographic trends of these changes are known so well that the industry plans with some confidence for conditions which will exist ten and twenty years hence. The changes in oil geography will be faster and more extensive, but again are known in broader outline. Whatever the changes are, it will be very exceptionally and locally, and only for certain minerals, that changes in distribution of production will be sufficient to invalidate for decades to come the broad inferences which can now be drawn from the presently known facts.

Changes in the location of smelting, refining, and fabrication centers are likewise in generally known directions. On the whole they are even slower than changes in the distribution of mineral production because of the inertia of invested capital, and difficulty of moving vast assemblages of coordinated plants and industries. The improvement of transportation facilities makes it easier to reach out for raw materials to the far quarters of the globe, even for such bulky minerals as iron ore.

Chapter III

THE MINERAL POSITION OF THE NATIONS

THE relative positions occupied by the nations of the world as regards the possession of mineral wealth can be concisely stated in statistical tables, and in the short period since the war these have become available for most of the world for the first time.[1] Few people, however, care to take the time or

[1] General statistical sources most available to the American reader are:

"The Mineral Resources of the United States" (annual publication), U. S. Bur. Mines, Washington, D. C.

Mineral Raw Materials, Trade Promotion Series, No. 76, Bur. Foreign and Domestic Commerce, Washington, D. C., 1929.

Summarized data of copper, zinc, lead, and gold production, Economic Papers, U. S. Bur. Mines, Washington, D. C.

"World Atlas of Commercial Geology," Part I, Distribution of Mineral Production, U. S. Geol. Survey, Washington, D. C., 1921.

"The Mineral Industry" (annual publication), McGraw-Hill Book Company, Inc., New York.

Year Book of the American Bureau of Metal Statistics (annual publication), New York.

Reports of the Imperial Institute (formerly Imperial Mineral Resources Bureau), London.

"The Iron Ore Resources of the World," XI Intern. Geol. Congr., Stockholm, 1910, 2 volumes, with atlas.

"The Coal Resources of the World," XII Intern. Geol. Congr., Toronto, 1913, 3 volumes, with atlas.

Reports of the Committee on Foreign and Domestic Mining Policy of the Mining and Met. Soc. of Am. (see Appendix B).

have the technical background to interpret such tables. We shall therefore present the situation qualitatively in the hope of making a readable story. Many qualifications and details must necessarily be eliminated to accomplish this purpose.

By what mineral standards should nations be ranked? What minerals, out of the very long list of those entering into commerce, are essential to large industrial development or to the maintenance of agriculture?

First in importance clearly stand the mineral fuels and iron ore. The industrial position of a nation may be very well gauged by its consumption of power, which in turn is a function of the use of machines and fuels. Consequently it is hard to over-emphasize the importance of iron products out of which machines are made, and of the mineral fuels which propel them. In 1928 the value of the world's pig-iron production was three and a half times that of gold, and that of fuels was thirteen times as great.

Second in importance is the group of copper, lead, and zinc used in commerce in large bulk. With these should probably be ranked the fertilizer group of minerals—phosphate, potash, and nitrate (natural or synthetic), together with sulphur used so largely in preparing fertilizers as well as in a vast range of manufacturing and refining operations.

[46]

No other mineral groups are so vital to national power and welfare as the foregoing, though others may of course constitute valuable assets. Industrial power cannot be built up on gold and silver. There is a long list of minerals used in minor quantities in the making of iron and steel, including nickel, manganese, chromite, fluorspar, vanadium, tungsten, and others. No one of these minerals and no combination of them is a basis for industrial development. Because of the relatively small quantities needed they may be transported from far parts of the world to the industrial centers. Access to such minerals is necessary to countries with heavy industries, and their control is a matter of international concern. Much the same remarks can be made about asbestos, mica, mercury, graphite, antimony, and tin. The mineral standing of countries can therefore be ranked principally on the basis of the two groups named in the preceding paragraphs.

A well-balanced supply of the vital minerals affords a firmer basis for industry than the possession of one or a few of them in very large amounts. Countries possessing the secondary minerals must be given a lower ranking on the ground that no combination of these minerals will yield industrial power and that they will be tributary to the industry based on the first two groups. Experience has shown that the commercial advantage accruing to the country of origin is far less than that gained where the minerals are consumed as well as possessed.

This discussion makes no reference to water, which from some points of view should be put at the head of the mineral list. Its story, however, is a separate one. Water is another environmental factor like soil, climate, and geography, influencing all human activities.

The United States

From almost any point of view the United States is the outstanding mineral country. It is the largest owner, the largest producer, and the largest consumer of minerals. In all three ways the United States accounts for about 40 per cent of the world's totals—for some minerals, of course, much less than this, for others more. It is the only country in the world possessing adequate quantities of nearly all the principal industrial minerals and leads the world in the production of coal, oil, natural gas, iron, copper, lead, zinc, aluminum metal, phosphates, gypsum, and sulphur. It also leads in the production of some minor minerals—arsenic, borax, cadmium, molybdenum, and talc. Nowhere else are the principal minerals grouped in such adequate quantities.

The output of energy in the United States from coal, oil, natural gas, and water power amounts to nearly half of the world's total. The total power available from man and beasts being insignificant in comparison, it is not far out of the way to state that the United States today is actually doing nearly half of the world's work. For a long time in the early stages of the industrial revolution Great Britain held a preeminent position in output of energy. In 1870 it was releasing about three times as much energy as the United States. Now the ratio is reversed, the United States producing three times that of Great Britain. The two curves of production crossed about the opening of the century, but the significance of the crossing was hardly realized at that time. In fact, even now it is common to assume that this country owes much of its commercial prominence to the war, without taking into account the fact that energy output (which is one of the truest measurements of wealth) has been rising on a generally predictable curve for the last sixty years, regardless of war and financial disturbances.

The only minerals available in the United States in large quantities for export are coal, phosphates, and sulphur, but if we add to its totals the minerals which it controls commercially in other countries, the United States exports copper, oil, zinc, and silver.

Notwithstanding its highly favored position, the United States depends almost entirely on foreign sources for several important minerals: antimony, chromite, manganese, nickel, tin, asbestos, bauxite, nitrates, platinum, and potash, and it is very largely dependent on foreign sources also for mercury, tungsten, barite, china clay, fluorspar, graphite, magnesite, mica, and pyrite. There are some supplementary imports of certain of the minerals, iron ore, for instance, which the United States possesses in adequate amounts, for the reason that delivery from abroad may be cheaper to certain plants than delivery from domestic points. Also for some minerals possessed in adequate amounts for our own use, like oil and copper, there are imports which more or less balance exports. In other words, the United States draws in crude supplies of these substances and sends them out again, usually after processing.

Looking into the future and taking account of increased consumption and diminishing sources of supply, we may conclude that before very long it will be necessary for us—to meet our own needs alone—to draw on the rest of the world for increasing quantities of oil, copper, iron, lead, and a number of other minerals which we use in smaller quantities.

Of the fertilizer minerals the United States possesses only phosphates and sulphur in adequate quantities. As yet the United States is dependent on Chile for much of its nitrate, but this dependence is being reduced with the development of the synthetic nitrate industry. Potash is imported from

Germany and France to the extent of about five times the domestic production, but development of domestic sources promises some reduction in this percentage.

Especially notable is the deficiency of the United States in some of the common ferro-alloy minerals necessary in the making of steel, particularly manganese, chromite, nickel, and vanadium. These are in the list classed as "key" minerals in war time.

It is natural that a mineral industry as large and thriving as that of the United States should undertake mineral exploitation in other parts of the world. Political or national considerations so prominent in this effort in other countries (particularly Great Britain) are secondary influences with the American mineral industry. It is primarily a question of commercial demand and profit. Among the important minerals outside of the United States, in which American commercial interests share largely in control, are copper in Chile, Peru, Canada, and Rhodesia; vanadium in Peru; tin in Bolivia; iron ore in Cuba, Chile, and Brazil; oil in Mexico, Venezuela, and other South American countries; oil in the Dutch East Indies; oil in Mesopotamia, in joint control with Great Britain, France, and the Netherlands through the Turkish Petroleum Company; zinc in Canada, Newfoundland, Mexico, Peru, and Poland; asbestos in Canada; gypsum in Canada; manganese in Brazil; chromite in Cuba,

Canada, and Brazil; aluminum in British and Dutch Guiana and in Europe. American activity in the acquisition of minerals outside of the boundaries of the United States is on the increase. By far the larger part of the world's exploitation of mineral resources is now in the hands of the United States and Great Britain.

Canada

Canada produces almost all the world's nickel, and exports substantial quantities of gold, silver, lead, copper, zinc, asbestos, cobalt, and gypsum. Formerly it largely monopolized the asbestos market of the world but is now giving way to South Africa as regards the higher grades. It lacks in whole or in large part iron ore, oil, tin, nitrates, potash, and most of the ferro-alloy minerals. Its principal weakness is the absence of iron ore. The imports of iron ore and iron and steel products into Canada each year are about equivalent to the country's entire mineral production. Canada also imports nearly all of its oil. About half of its coal is imported, not because it does not possess coal—its reserves are very large—but because much of the developed coal is not of the best grade and is located principally in Alberta and Nova Scotia, whence the cost of transportation to the principal consuming centers in Ontario is greater than the cost of importing coal from the United States. A larger use of domestic coal is to be expected in the future. Canada's total mineral production is about 4 per cent of that of the United States, and its production of the non-ferrous metals is about 28 per cent of that of the United States.

Canada is of special interest in that it contains one of the world's potentially largest mineralized areas, as yet undeveloped. Exploration is going on here on a larger scale than almost anywhere else in the world, and discoveries are relatively frequent. The best outlook seems to be in the field of non-ferrous metals; there is comparatively little promise of improvement in the oil and iron ore situations. Copper and platinum, now being developed in Sudbury nickel mines, will be important factors. Very little Canadian capital goes out of the country for mineral exploitation, but nearly half of the country's own production is controlled commercially by the United States and Great Britain.

The Canadian government is taking an increasingly active part not only in exploration but in the mineral industry. A strong effort is being made to build up Canadian smelters and manufactures with a view to changing the position of the country from that of contributor of raw materials to one of industrial independence. The situation is of special interest from a world standpoint because of Canada's position between the two great exploiting countries of the world (the United States and Great

Britain), which are in active competition to acquire her minerals. The question as to their ultimate control affords a good illustration of the general world problem.[1]

Mexico

Mexico's mineral consumption is small and a considerable part of all the minerals mined is available for export. The principal silver production of the world comes from Mexico. Other important contributions are oil, lead, zinc, gold, copper, antimony, arsenic, and graphite. For a time Mexico was second in the world in oil production, but failed to conduct explorations to keep up with production. Coal is lacking in adequate amounts and good grades. Iron ore exists in scattered deposits of considerable size but is not likely to be utilized for some years because of geographic distribution and somewhat undesirable grade. There is little chance for large industrial development under these circumstances. Further discoveries are likely in the group of non-ferrous minerals.

Mexico's minerals are dominated by outside capital, principally American and British, and in general serve as feeders to the established mineral industries of these two countries.

[1] LEITH, C. K., Canada's Minerals and Their International Implications, *Mining Met.*, pp. 463–467, October, 1929.

South America

South America has a very small consumption of minerals, and practically all those produced go to the principal industrial centers of the North Atlantic countries. Nowhere in South America is there a combination of essential minerals necessary for great industrial development. The greatest lack is coal. Only in Chile, Peru, Brazil, and Colombia are there coal reserves, and these are of such low grade that they are not suitable for important use. Mineral output is in many scattered units, not integrated with one another, but with North Atlantic industries. Among the most important is the nitrate of Chile, which is almost the world's exclusive source of natural nitrate. Copper is exported in large quantities from Chile and Peru. Peru has the largest and best vanadium deposit of the world and also contributes lead and silver in minor amounts. The production of oil is important in South America and is gaining rapidly. At present Venezuela is second only to the United States in its oil production, but there are important contributions also from Peru, Colombia, Trinidad, Ecuador, and Argentina. It is expected that these will increase as exploration and development proceed. Iron ore exists in important amounts in Brazil, and in smaller scattered deposits in Chile, Venezuela, and elsewhere. Iron ores from Chile are now being shipped

to the United States, and in the near future will
be exported to North Atlantic points from Brazil.
Other minerals being produced on a world scale
by various South American countries include the tin
of Bolivia (23 per cent of the world total), platinum
from Colombia (28 per cent), bauxite from the
British and Dutch Guianas (25 per cent), and
manganese from Brazil (8 per cent).

Nearly all of the South American governments
are making an effort to tighten their hold on mineral
resources, as a defensive reaction against the
exploitation of their countries by United States
and European capital, but there is no indication
that the effort can anywhere result in complete
independence. South America as a whole is likely
to remain essentially a feeder of raw materials to
the great industrial centers of the world.

Great Britain and the British Empire[1]

Great Britain is the great competitor of the United
States in control of the world's minerals, but within
its own boundaries it has but few minerals. It
has less than adequate quantities of lead, tin,
barite, and gypsum. It almost completely lacks
aluminum, antimony, chromite, copper, manganese, mercury, nickel, tungsten, zinc, asbestos,
graphite, magnesite, mica, nitrates, petroleum,

[1] Canada, Australia, and Africa are discussed under separate head-
ings (pages 52, 67), but a general view is here given.

phosphates, potash, pyrites, sulphur, talc, and soapstone. Of the few minerals it possesses, only coal, fluorspar, and china clay figure largely in export. The iron ore, while abundant, is of low grade and even for domestic consumption must be supplemented by importation of high-grade ores to the extent of nearly half (in metallic content) of the local production. British coal, by virtue of its high grade, its proximity to the coast, and the fact that Great Britain is so largely a maritime nation, has in the past figured more largely in international trade than any other mineral commodity. For a long time it made up about two-thirds of the total tonnage of British exports, and was therefore the principal balance for the necessary large imports of other raw materials. England still leads the world in its export of coal, but it is losing its preeminent position because of increased competition from without and increased cost at home.

If all the mineral resources of the British Empire were considered as a single group the combination would be a very strong one, probably superior to that of the United States. It would lack only such minor minerals as antimony, potash, mercury, sulphur, talc, soapstone, nitrates, barite, and magnesite, and its oil resources might be inadequate. A notable fact is the British Empire's commercial control of more than 70 per cent of the world's gold production. It produces more than 43 per cent of

[57]

the world's tin, and through smelters and refineries commercially controlled by its nationals handles slightly more than 80 per cent of the world's total.

The striking feature of the British mineral position is the activity of capital, for many decades past, in acquiring control of needed minerals in other parts of the world, particularly in the British Empire. The incentive has been primarily commercial, as in the United States, but in recent years national and political motives have come to play a part. One of the conspicuous results of this effort has been the acquirement of oil (see page 87).

Continental Europe

If all the mineral resources of continental Europe were pooled they would rank in variety and abundance with those of the United States. There would still be deficiencies in copper, lead, and zinc, which the United States has in abundance. On the other hand, Europe has supplies of potash, mercury, and manganese, which are missing in the United States. Like the United States, it must go to other parts of the world for its tin, nickel, and nitrates. The minerals of Europe are handicapped in competition with the United States by the fact that they are divided among many small competing commercial organizations and by political barriers (particularly tariffs) set up in the way of their common use. Pooling of interests in one form or another is here and there bringing together the

[58]

mineral industries of the various countries and the process is likely to go farther. A notable instance is the rapid advance of the European iron and steel industry through mutual understandings and co-operative arrangements.

A striking feature of post-war changes in the European mineral situation has been the tendency to restore the pre-war functioning of the industries based on natural groupings of raw materials, regardless of new political lines. The political dismemberment of these groups under the Peace Treaty has proved, on the whole, a commercial failure. Much needless loss and friction might have been avoided if the distribution of raw materials and the industries based upon them had been taken into account when the terms of peace were settled, instead of the consideration solely of the racial, linguistic, historical, and geographic conditions. Political adjustment to remedy this mistake is already in evidence.

The great part played in human history by Mediterranean peoples has led in some quarters to the hope of a rejuvenation along western industrial lines. But whatever advances may be made in other fields of activity as regards mineral resources, there is nothing in this entire region that promises anything like the industrial development of middle Europe and the United States. Especially notable are its deficiencies in coal and iron, to say nothing of many other important minerals. Whatever advances are made in the future must be on lines other than those of the great industrial revolution based primarily on adequate mineral supplies.

Let us now take up some of the principal countries of Europe more specifically.

France.—Within its own boundaries France has large quantities of bauxite (aluminum ore), iron ore, gypsum, potash (Alsace), talc, and soapstone, but is preeminent only in the production of bauxite. It almost completely lacks asbestos, chromite, copper, lead, manganese, mercury, nickel, tin, tungsten, zinc, graphite, mica, nitrates, petroleum, magnesite, fluorspar, and sulphur. Also, domestic supplies must be largely supplemented by imports of antimony, barite, china clay, coal, phosphates, and pyrite. The outstanding deficiencies from the industrial standpoint are the limited supplies of coal of a proper coking grade, and of oil, copper, lead, and zinc. The deficiency in iron ore has now been made up by the acquisition of Lorraine. French capital has purchased the majority of the properties owned by Germans. Efforts to secure supplies outside the boundaries of France have been largely confined to the French colonies and mandates. In this way France has acquired an exportable surplus of chromite and nickel from New Caledonia, graphite from Madagascar, and phosphates from North Africa, and has made up part of its deficiency in iron, manganese, lead, and zinc from North Africa.

Germany.—Within its own boundaries Germany has an abundance only of non-metallic minerals—coal, barite, fluorspar, gypsum, nitrates, and potash. Coal and potash are the outstanding assets. Germany's potash is almost a world monopoly, and coal is the basis of its great industrial development, principally in the Ruhr valley. Germany needs large supplementary imports of copper, iron, lead, china clay, graphite, mica, talc, and soapstone. Minerals almost completely lacking make a formidable list—bauxite, antimony, chromite, manganese, mercury, nickel, tin, tungsten, zinc, asbestos, magnesite, petroleum, phosphates, pyrite, and sulphur. There is some possibility that exploration now under way will supply the deficiency in oil. No other large industrial nation has so small a control of essential minerals either at home or abroad.

Notwithstanding Germany's many mineral deficiencies, its possession of coal and iron enabled it before the war to build up an iron and steel industry second only to that of the United States, and, through its smelting, refining, and manufacturing capacity, to exercise considerable control on the flow of world minerals. As a result of the war it lost all but an insignificant part of its iron ores, its principal lead and zinc ores, and an important but not the larger part of its coal. Also, its commercial control of zinc ore from Broken Hill, Australia, was disrupted, and this flow of zinc was deflected to England and Belgium.

Since the war Germany has started with its usual energy and skill to restore its manufacturing and smelting enterprises on the basis of foreign supplies of minerals. Already the pre-war scale of importation has been reached or surpassed for antimony, asbestos, bauxite, chrome ore, copper, gypsum, iron ore, nickel, pyrite, quicksilver, sulphur, and tin. Importations of lead, manganese, and zinc, however, are still far under the pre-war scale. It is an interesting question for the future whether the possession of coal, together with manufacturing plant, organizing power, and enterprise, will be sufficient for Germany to overcome deficiencies in raw materials. Production of pig iron and steel is now approaching pre-war figures. In 1923 and 1924 France, including the Saar, surpassed Germany in pig-iron production and has almost equaled Germany since. In those years it also almost equaled Germany in steel production, but since then has fallen behind. The center of gravity of the great iron and steel industry of western Europe is shifting back to Germany and the shift will be more obvious if the Saar is returned. In all steel industries the supply of coking coal has determined the center of manufacture.

The first and most important step in rehabilitation is now being taken, namely, the reaching of commercial and political agreements with France and Poland to restore the efficiency of the industries based on the resources formerly controlled by Germany. The Lorraine iron ore and the Ruhr coal, with the complementary German and French smelting and manufacturing plants, constitute a great natural unit, the dominant industry of western Europe, no part of which can be operated to best advantage without the rest. Much the same is true of the German-Polish zinc industry. World competition is forcing cooperation, and this requires the lowering of political barriers.

Belgium.—The only minerals within the boundaries of Belgium in quantity are iron, barite, coal, and phosphates, and these exist in inadequate amounts which must be largely supplemented by imports. Belgium's commercial control outside its boundaries has been extended mainly to copper, cobalt, and tin in the Congo. Through its possessions in the Congo and its domestic reduction facilities, Belgium is becoming self-sustaining in tin and is materially increasing its exportable surplus. Through its activities in smelting zinc ores from foreign sources it has made itself the world's principal exporter of zinc metal and principal broker in the world's zinc market.

[63]

Spain.—Spain has an exportable surplus of copper, iron, lead, zinc, manganese, mercury, and pyrite, and adequate amounts for its own use of tungsten, barite, fluorspar, graphite, gypsum, talc, and soapstone. Its domestic consumption is small. Its iron ore production is dwindling. Together with Italy it produces most of the world's mercury. For the rest, its minerals are in inadequate amounts or entirely lacking. Vital deficiencies are coal and oil. British capital dominates most of the Spanish minerals.

Spain's only effort to develop minerals outside of its boundaries is in Spanish Morocco, and even there this activity is left largely to other nations. Iron ore is its principal development thus far.

Italy.—Italy has an exportable surplus in aluminum, mercury, zinc, barite, graphite, sulphur, talc, and soapstone, but its only world leadership—that in mercury—is shared with Spain. It has quantities sufficient for its own limited use of iron, lead, fluorspar, gypsum, potash, and pyrite. Other minerals are entirely lacking or are present in inadequate amounts.

The Italians are not active in exploration for minerals, though they are now putting forth some effort in their own colonies in North Africa. There is evidence that the present Italian government is giving much more attention to this subject than formerly.

Sweden and Norway.—Outside of large quantities of high-grade iron ore in Sweden, of great importance to the future of the European steel industry, the Scandinavian countries do not possess minerals of great consequence in world perspective. Their nationals show little activity outside their own boundaries.

Sweden produces a large exportable surplus of iron ore and a small surplus of zinc ore and cement, sufficient manganese and feldspar to meet its own requirements, and almost enough lead, but is forced to rely on imports for all the other minerals.

Norway exports its surplus of titanium, magnesite, iron ore, talc, feldspar, and pyrite, much of which is copper bearing, and the local demand for silver, molybdenite, and nickel is met by the domestic supplies, but the remaining minerals are imported. A deposit of bauxite on one of the Norwegian islands in the Arctic Ocean has been announced recently, which may make the aluminum industry of Norway independent of foreign ores.

Poland.—Poland as a mineral producer figures in coal, zinc, potash, and an iron and steel industry based primarily on its possession of coal, together with iron ore deposits of small size within its own boundaries. Although Poland produces less than 1 per cent of the world's oil, the local consumption is so small that petroleum products are exported. The requirements for lead are supplied from within

[65]

the country and about a half of the demand for potash. Poland's present mineral position is largely due to acquisition of part of Silesia from Germany.

Czechoslovakia.—Czechoslovakia is the world's principal producer of graphite, and is favored by the possession of adequate supplies of coal and iron, largely taken over from Austria. The iron ore deposits, while fairly large, are of rather low grade, and high-grade ores from Sweden and Spain are imported in order to raise the iron content of the mixture. Czechoslovakia also has sufficient antimony and mercury for small exports.

Russia.—Russia has a large exportable surplus of platinum, manganese, and petroleum. Together with Colombia it now dominates the world's platinum market. It exports about 8 per cent of the world's graphite and a small amount of coal. Its supplies of coal, iron, pyrite, gold, asbestos, salt, and chromite are adequate for domestic consumption. Copper, lead, zinc, and other minerals are known in minor amounts. The vast extent of Russia's unexplored country, together with low consumption of minerals, make it difficult to appraise her future position in world mineral production. Production is rapidly increasing under the "Five-year Plan," but as yet there is little indication of developments in excess of its own growing needs, except for the minerals first named. Recent exports of certain minerals at the expense of domestic needs are not a sound basis for assuming future surplus. Russia has practically no control of minerals outside of its own territory.

Africa

Africa's outstanding contributions have been the gold and diamonds of South Africa, both of which dominate the world production. Rhodesia produces about half of the world's chromite. Other important contributions have been copper in the Congo, lead and zinc in Algeria, tin in Nigeria, manganese in the Gold Coast and Egypt, phosphates in Tunisia, Morocco, and Algeria, and graphite in Madagascar. Coal and iron in adequate amounts seem to exist only in the Union of South Africa, where there is promise of a self-sustaining iron and steel industry sufficient to meet local needs. Smaller iron ore supplies exist in Tunisia, Algeria, and Morocco, where they are mined for export. Still others are reported from various sources, but none of known importance. Oil production is now confined to Egypt, and Africa as a whole does not yet promise large production for the future. Copper development in the Congo and Rhodesia, however, is coming forward rapidly, and it is not impossible that this may prove to be the world's largest future source of copper. Other developments anticipated for the future are increases in the production of manganese in the Gold Coast and South Africa,

[67]

of tin in Nigeria, of chromite, asbestos, and platinum in South Africa, and of graphite in Madagascar.

The minerals of Africa are dominated by British and European capital, and American capital figures largely only in the Rhodesian coppers. Local consumption being insignificant, all minerals move toward North Atlantic industrial centers. Africa, like Canada and South America, is the battlefield of competing exploitation by North Atlantic interests. The only part of Africa which seems to have the raw materials necessary for an independent industrial development is the Union of South Africa.

Most of Africa, unlike South America, is controlled politically by the same countries from which the forces of exploitation originate, and there are many interesting political aspects of the competition for the control of raw materials.

Australia

Australia produces a considerable variety of minerals but none of them figures largely in world production, except lead, zinc, gold, and silver. Formerly it was a larger producer of both gold and silver, but its output has now fallen off. It is dependent on outside sources for its petroleum. Coal and iron exist in adequate amounts and the iron and steel industry of New South Wales is approaching a position where it can take care of

Australian requirements. Iron ore is being exported to Japan and the United States.

Australian minerals are largely controlled by English capital, but the Australian government is taking active steps to make the country industrially independent and to divert its minerals to its own industries.

The Far East

It is a common belief that large undeveloped mineral resources exist in the Far East, but this is hardly justified by the facts. In discussions of the "challenge of Asia," the "awakening of the Far East," and the "yellow peril" there is usually either an expressed or a concealed assumption that the resources are there for industrial development when the time comes. This assumption has been questioned by mineral specialists who, from various studies, have agreed that while important mineral deposits exist, they are of a variety and are so distributed that they seem to offer little chance for a large industrial development.[1]

The Far East produces a rather imposing aggregate of minerals, although it is far short of the total produced either in the United States or in Europe. However, the sources are scattered among so many

[1] BAIN, H. FOSTER, " Ores and Industry in the Far East," Council on Foreign Relations, New York, 1927. LEITH, C. K., The Mineral Resources of the Far East, *Foreign Affairs*, vol. 4, No. 3, pp. 433-442, April, 1926.

nations that they do not constitute an adequate basis for independent industrial development. Local consumption is small. A very large part of the mineral production of the Far East therefore flows toward the North Atlantic and is controlled by the industries of that region.

China meets the largest part of the world's requirements for two minor minerals—tungsten and antimony, and also produces an appreciable amount of tin. Lead, zinc, tin, tungsten, oil, and silver are contributed by Burma but only to a minor extent on the world scale. Japanese copper production meets the local demands, but the iron ores are inadequate. Manchuria produces small amounts of coal and iron. The Malay Peninsula and adjacent parts of the Dutch East Indies dominate the world's tin production with 55.6 per cent of the total. The Dutch East Indies contribute 2.6 per cent of the world's petroleum. India holds first place in the world's production of high-grade manganese ore 35 per cent of total, and of sheet mica (65 per cent). Something less than 6 per cent of the world's gold comes from India, Korea, Japan, China, and the East Indies, combined.

The key to the industrial situation is the question of coal and iron. Japan, with the best organization, industrial development, and consuming power, has little coal and iron within its own boundaries, and is attempting to make up its deficiency by the development of coal and iron in Manchuria. The coal supply is large, but not of the best grade. The Manchurian iron ore is extremely low grade, requiring beneficiation. Commercial success is as yet doubtful. In the meantime Japan has brought in iron ore in small quantities from Korea, China, Malay, and now from Australia. China has plenty of high-grade coal, but insufficient iron ore, and has other industrial minerals in adequate amounts. India has an abundance of high-grade iron ore but only a limited supply of coal of proper coking quality. The Philippines and the Dutch East Indies have large reserves of medium-grade iron ore of a mineral content which causes difficulties in smelting, but they have no large amounts of coking coal. If the coal of north-eastern China could be brought together with the high-grade iron ores of India and possibly with the iron ores of the Philippines and the Dutch East Indies a large industrial advance might be possible. The distances might not prove insuperable obstacles in these days of improved transportation. Iron ore is now being moved from Australia to Japan and from Chile to the United States, and there are many other examples of long-distance hauls of minerals in great bulk. But the political difficulties involved are not likely to be surmounted for a long time to come.

The rôle of the Far East is therefore likely to remain essentially that of a contributor of a few minerals from scattered sources to the North Atlantic

industries and exploited and controlled from these
sources. Only in a small way will independence
develop to meet slowly increasing local needs, as,
for instance, the iron and steel industry of India and
such industry as Japan may be able to develop under
highly disadvantageous conditions, both physical
and political, by drawing in supplies from far-distant
sources. Nevertheless it should be noted that the
pooling of the mineral resources of all the Far East,
such as they are, would probably do more toward
physical betterment of the Far Eastern peoples
than any other commercial measure now in sight.
The problem is a large and difficult one, both commercially and politically. Commercial interests
are already studying the problem and are even
making moves toward cooperation. On the other
hand, the political movement just at present is
toward disintegration. The political problem is
further referred to in later chapters.

The Situation Reviewed

The following table[1] summarizes graphically the
position of some of the consuming countries with
reference to the principal minerals. The black
dots indicate by their position the extent to which
the country in question is able to supply its needs of

[1] Adapted from Charts 1 and 2, FURNESS, J. W., and L. M. JONES,
Mineral Raw Materials, Trade Promotion Series, No. 76, Bur. Foreign
and Domestic Commerce, U. S. Dept. Commerce, pp. 4–7, 1929.

METALS AND THEIR ORES	UNITED STATES				GERMANY				FRANCE				U.KINGDOM				JAPAN				BELGIUM				ITALY				SPAIN			
	A	B	C	D	A	B	C	D	A	B	C	D	A	B	C	D	A	B	C	D	A	B	C	D	A	B	C	D	A	B	C	D
Aluminum	●					●			●						×					●				●	●							●
Antimony		●				●				●					×					●		●				●				●		
Chromite		●				●					×				×				●											●		
Copper	×	●				●	●	●		●			×		×			●						●				●	●			
Iron		●	●			●	●			●			×	●	×				●					●			●				●	
Lead		●				●	●			●				●	×				●					●		●				●		
Manganese			×				●	●							×					●				●				●				●
Mercury		●					●				×				×				●					●	●				●			
Nickel			●				●				×				×				●					●			●					●
Tin			●				●								×				●					●			●				●	
Tungsten		●				●				●					×				●			●				●				●		
Zinc	×	●				●				×			×		×				●					●			●				●	
NON-METALS																																
Asbestos	×					●				●			×						●		●					●				●		
Barite		●				●				●				×				●				●				●					●	
China Clay			●				●				×			●				●				●				●				●		
Coal	●					●				●			●						×		●					×			●			
Fluorspar		●				●				×				●					●			●				●				●		
Graphite		●				●				×				●					●			●			×					●		
Gypsum	●					●				●				×					●			●				●				●		
Magnesite			●				●			●				×				●					●				●				●	
Mica		●					●			●				×				●					●		●				●			
Nitrates			●				●			×				×					●			●				●			●			
Petroleum	×					●				×			×					●				●				●				●		
Phosphates	●					●				●				×					●			●				●				●		
Potash		●			●					●				×					●			●				●					●	
Pyrites		●				●				●				×					●			●				●			●			
Sulphur	●						●			×			×						●			●				●				●		
Talc and Soapstone		●					●			●				●					●			●				●				●		

A, Minerals available in large quantities for export. B, Minerals adequate to meet domestic demands without appreciable excess or deficiency. C, Minerals inadequate to meet domestic demands, partially dependent on foreign sources. D, Minerals for which the country depends almost entirely on foreign sources.

the mineral in question from within its own political boundaries; the crosses are used to indicate that the status of the country is improved when minerals under commercial or political control of that country, but situated outside its boundaries, are included with the domestic resources.

The mineral position of the nations presents several salient features.

1. The United States occupies a prominent position both as a consumer and as a producer of minerals from within its own boundaries, and as an active agent in mineral exploration and production in other countries.

2. Second in importance is the United Kingdom. It holds its position not by virtue of minerals within its boundaries, but by its wide financial control in other territories, particularly in the British Empire. United States and British capital together controls fully three-fourths of the world's mineral resources.

3. Third stands western Europe, if we consider it as a unit. No single European country has an outstanding group of mineral resources.

4. No other countries or groups control mineral supplies adequate for industrial development on a corresponding scale, notwithstanding their possession of large supplies of particular minerals. Such minerals as they have are mostly controlled by capital of North Atlantic countries and serve in the main as feeders to the industries of those countries.

South Africa, Russia, and Australia are the only outlying regions which have minerals adequate to permit the growth of independent industries. Asia has a possibility for industrial development if its widely scattered resources could be operated under unit control.

5. Exploitation of the world's minerals emanates from the industrial centers of the North Atlantic. In regard to mineral supplies there is no such thing as equality of nations. In so far as such supplies have contributed to the political and financial dominance of the North Atlantic countries in the past, there is no marked change in sight for the future.

6. Finally, not even the most favored nation is entirely self-sustaining in minerals, nor can it be made so. The interdependence of nations and specialization in mineral production have been determined once and for all by nature's distribution of minerals.

Chapter IV

WHAT THE NATIONS ARE DOING POLITICALLY

THE new mineral situation, as sketched in earlier chapters, has caused a quickening political consciousness of minerals the world over. The question of the political control of minerals has already emerged in some countries and for some minerals as one of major political importance, both from national and international viewpoints. No gift of prophecy is required to foresee it as one of the major political problems of the near future.

This subject is a highly complicated one with many rapidly shifting variables. Only a part of the information has yet been collected and analyzed, and any picture of the political situation must be broadly generalized. Nevertheless, a few salient trends are beginning to appear which seem to indicate with some certainty the crude outlines of future political problems.[1]

[1] Literature on this subject is too widely scattered for full reference, but the interested reader might start to advantage with the following discussions:

SPURR, J. E., editor, "Political and Commercial Geology," McGraw-Hill Book Company, Inc., New York, 1920.

SMITH, GEORGE OTIS, editor, "The Strategy of Minerals," D.

NATIONAL POLICIES

The first and most general of the political trends to be noted is the tightening of national political controls of mineral resources. The measures through which political control is exercised are immensely varied. Some are meant to aid and encourage private effort. Others are regulative and restrictive. Some touch the mineral industries lightly and indirectly. Others take direct control through regulation or

Appleton & Company, New York, 1919.

REQUA, MARK L., "The Relation of Government to Industry," The Macmillan Company, New York, 1925.

CULBERTSON, WILLIAM S., Raw Materials and Foodstuffs in the Commercial Policies of Nations, *Ann. Am. Acad. Polit. and Soc. Sci.*, vol. CXII, pp. 1–145, 1924.

Economic Tendencies Affecting the Peace of the World: Joint Memorandum by Professors J. BONN and ANDRE SIEGFRIED; Memorandum by Prof. J. BONN; and Memorandum by Prof. ANDRE SIEGFRIED, League of Nations, Geneva, 20 pp., April 9, 1929.

WALLACE, BENJAMIN B., and LYNN R. EDMINSTER, "International Control of Raw Materials," The Brookings Institution, Washington, 1930.

LEITH, C. K., "Economic Aspects of Geology," Henry Holt & Company, New York, 1921.

LEITH, C. K., Political Control of Mineral Resources, *Foreign Affairs*, vol. 3, pp. 541–555, 1925.

Report of the Federal Oil Conservation Board to the President of the United States, Government Printing Office, Washington, Part I, 1926; Part II, 1928; Part III, 1929.

Report of the United States Coal Commission (in five parts), *Senate Document* 195, sixty-eighth Congress, second session, Government Printing Office, Washington, 1925.

"International Control of Minerals," published jointly by Am. Inst. Mining Met. Eng. and Mining and Met. Soc. Am., New York, 1925 (see Appendix B).

even ownership and operation. Most of them are local or national in their scope, but a considerable body of international agreement has come into existence which in effect constitutes international political control. In a broad sense, resources are being nationalized. In some countries there has been nationalization in the narrower sense of taking over ownership, or operation, or both. In many mineral industries it is hard to draw a line between public and private control, as in the British-controlled oil industries.

The political trend is clearly toward national isolation and reflects the general post-war desire for national self-determination and equality of economic opportunity. The first political step, therefore, seems to oppose the tendency toward commercial integration of the world's mineral industries. From another point of view, however, it may be regarded as merely the natural preliminary step to more effective political adjustment to the commercial trend. As governments become more and more involved in the mineral business, the necessity for international movement of minerals determined by their primary distribution naturally draws the nations politically into understandings and agreements to make this movement possible.

Many of the political efforts toward national isolation are based on misconception of the natural resource situation and the extent to which it can be modified by political enactment. They therefore introduce much waste, expense, inefficiency, and friction. As the futility of such measures becomes obvious they are in time modified or abandoned in favor of measures which are better adapted to the physical and commercial realities.

The spread of national political controls often results from various local and special causes, but that there are more wide-spread and fundamental causes is signified by the fact that this movement began long before the war, was suddenly and largely advanced by the war, and has continued since the war, in all parts of the world, under a great variety of commercial and political conditions. It is a remarkable fact that hardly a single political step can be named, outside of the relinquishment of a few special war measures, in the direction of lessening political control of the mineral industry. There is no indication anywhere that this movement is yet losing its impetus. Inertia alone is sure to carry it farther even though causal conditions should begin to change.

The motives of this great political movement vary widely in time and place, but common among them are the fear of future shortage, the fear of being crowded into disadvantageous commercial position by other nations, the fear of being caught without supplies in case of war, the desire to secure and retain markets for mineral surplus, and the desire in general to get as large a return to the nation as is possible, through development and royalties, and through encouragement to smelting and manufacturing designed to keep the profit at home. In normal times the world produces enough of all minerals to supply all nations, and the dominant problem is one of maintaining production and markets under competition, but the experience of the last war shows how easy it is to deprive nations of needed supplies by war measures or by centralization of commercial and political control. Nations possessing key minerals are coming to realize how they may be used, under strong commercial and political control, as trading assets, either in war or in peace, to secure other raw materials which are lacking. Whatever the motives or justification, the desire for national protection in regard to mineral supplies has become almost an obsession with many nations.

Keeping in mind the general nature of the political trends above sketched, we may briefly review some of the specific policies of the nations.

The United States

In the United States there has been less political control of minerals than in any of the principal mineral-bearing nations. Private capital and initiative have been given almost full sway in development of the mineral industry. Yet as the situation is examined more closely there may be noted a considerable number of evidences of increasing political attention to the problem. After about nine-tenths of the public domain had been alienated from the government, a leasing law was enacted ("United States General Leasing Act of 1920") for the remaining one-tenth, putting marked restrictions on the freedom of development and acquirement of mineral resources by private capital. This applies to public lands carrying coal, petroleum, oil shale, phosphates, and potassium and sodium salts. Ownership of the minerals was retained by the government and private capital allowed access to them only in limited areas and by the payment of royalties to the government. Before and since there have been further special withdrawals of minerals and mineral lands, such as potash, oil for naval purposes, helium for dirigibles, and others. The present temper of the public with reference to the alienation of mineral lands has been shown unmistakably in the naval oil scandals. An amendment (1930) to the Leasing Act permits lessees of government lands to participate in unit operations of oil pools (see pages 136–137).

In the Leasing Act also there is a provision against the free participation of foreigners in the exploitation of our minerals, it being provided that extra-nationals shall not participate if their countries exclude Americans from participation.

The state of Minnesota now imposes such restrictions that comparatively few new leases on state iron ore lands have been made in recent years.

The acquisition of mineral deposits in the Philippines is limited to Filipinos and American citizens. Also, coal can be mined only by leasing from the government. Still further, the Phillipine government has taken direct financial participation in a company organized to develop coal resources.

Under the great land grants formerly given to railway and other companies actual issuance of patents in recent years has been surrounded by many technical restrictions where the lands are suspected of carrying minerals. Suits have been brought by the government, as in the case of the Southern Pacific Railway, for the recovery of minerals on lands previously patented under a land grant.

Attempts have been made under the Sherman and Clayton Acts and by state anti-trust legislation to prevent anything approaching monopoly. As commercial units of the mineral industry grow in size by merger, they are being more closely scrutinized and tested than ever before to make sure that they will not create monopolies. This situation is undoubtedly holding back certain super-combinations which would in effect bring about this result. The United States also took legal action under the anti-trust laws against the Franco-

German potash combination, winning a hollow victory. Still further the State Department has discouraged loans to the German potash industry and other foreign monopolies of raw materials. The problem is yet to be settled how far monopoly of minerals is to be allowed to go, and, if it becomes inevitable, how it shall be controlled by government.

In the coal situation the government has stepped in twice through commissions, with various suggestions of a larger measure of public control. Much the same has been done with oil. The restriction of oil production now under way was suggested by the Federal Oil Conservation Board and is being in part carried out through the intervention of state governments.

Public discussions of coal and oil contain more and more references to the possibility of nationalization as a panacea. In coal, particularly, nationalization has been put forward by radical political parties and in measures brought before Congress.

Less obvious as measures of widening public control but not to be overlooked are taxes and tariffs. Some of our minerals are now carrying heavy burdens of state taxation over and above those imposed on other business, on the specified or implied ground that the minerals really belong to the people, and, if allowed to remain in private ownership, should make special contributions to tax funds. Taxation of this kind is undoubtedly affecting the distribution of iron ore production in the Lake Superior region. Others to be mentioned are the anthracite tax in Pennsylvania (soon to run out), the Texas and Louisiana taxes on oil and sulphur, the Alabama tax on coal and iron ore, and the Montana tax on coal and oil. Tariffs of growing number and size are being placed on mineral imports as a means of aiding and developing new mineral industries to make the country self-sustaining. Export taxes are unconstitutional.

In a few cases the government has participated directly in mineral development, as in drilling for potash now under way in the Permian basin of Texas and adjacent states, production of helium for naval purposes, and others.

Abroad our mineral industries have, on the whole, been allowed to shift for themselves, and with their great commercial power they have been able to manage it, but as foreign countries have built up political obstacles to these activities the American government has been called on more and more frequently to aid in surmounting them. Our insistence on the policy of the "open door" has had wide application to the field of mineral exploration and development. The participation of our oil interests in the Turkish Petroleum Company operating in Mesopotamia was made possible only by active intervention of the American government.

Under the provisions of the exclusion clause in our Leasing Act of 1920, reciprocal arrangements have now been completed with the Netherlands government whereby Americans may explore in the Dutch East Indies, in return for like privilege to Netherlands' citizens in the United States. Similar arrangements may be made with other countries as needed.

Our treaty with Germany of 1923 provides that:

The nationals of either High Contracting Party shall, moreover, enjoy within the territories of the other, reciprocally and upon compliance with the conditions there imposed, such rights and privileges as have been or may hereafter be accorded the nationals of any other state with respect to the mining of coal, phosphate, oil, oil shale, gas, and sodium on the public domain of the other.

This treaty is now used as a model for all United States commercial treaties. Treaties containing the clause quoted have been negotiated with Austria, Esthonia, Honduras, Hungary, and Latvia.

Aid has been given to the mineral industries also by allowing them to combine for foreign trade under the Webb Export Trade Act of 1918. The Copper Exporters, Inc., including foreign non-voting membership, controls 90 per cent of the world's copper export sales. The Sulphur Exporters Association, Inc., by agreement with Sicilian interests, controls the world's sulphur exports. The Export Petroleum

[85]

Association, Inc., with foreign participation, aims to unify the export market in oil and oil products.

The British Empire

In the United Kingdom nationalization of coal has been a major political issue in recent years.[1] The government has now assumed control over the coal-mining industry, under which the production of each district will be rationed by a committee of mine owners, whose actions must be approved by the Board of Trade. Outside of the United Kingdom, the British government exercises a wide range of control over minerals, both directly and through dominion and colonial governments. In most of the Empire, excepting Malay, under direct control of the British government there are restrictions against alien exploration and acquirement of minerals, particularly oil—in some places under general laws and in others through a considerable variety of enactments, orders, and rulings of political subdivisions. This extends in practice even to mandated territory, notwithstanding provision to the contrary in the Covenant of the League of Nations, and has been the subject of protest at Geneva. Americans are excepted by reciprocal arrangements under provisions of the U. S. Leasing Act of 1920. For Burma, no

[1] Report of the Royal Commission on the Coal Industry (1925), London, 1926. See also: "Coal and Power," the Report of an Enquiry presided over by the Right Hon. D. Lloyd George, Hodder & Stoughton, London, 1924.

reciprocal arrangement with the United States has yet been made.

Direct participation of the British government in the mineral industry now reaches a rather imposing total. The government is a partner in the Anglo-Persian Oil Company, which operates as a producing company and has joint holdings with the Australian government in the Commonwealth Refinery. It is a partner of Australia—in the development of oil resources of Papua (New Guinea), with the Egyptian government in oil exploration in Egypt, and with Australia and New Zealand in mining phosphates in the Island of Nauru. Both Papua and Nauru are mandated territories. The government exercises some degree of indirect control also through companies such as the British South Africa Company. The specific relations of the government to these companies are widely various and in some cases are not fully known to the public.

The activity of the British government is especially conspicuous in oil. The key position of oil became apparent in the World War, when it began to be substituted in large quantities for coal in steamships. The British government then made it a state policy to acquire oil reserves for the future, and aided its commercial interests with a variety of political measures. It owns the majority of shares in the Anglo-Persian Company, and requires that the control of operations of the Turkish Petroleum

Company shall be British. It is closely affiliated with the Royal Dutch Shell. The campaign has been highly successful. It is estimated that Great Britain now controls almost as much of the world's future reserves as does the United States, though still far short of the United States in production.

Political control has been maintained over the tin industry of Malay and Nigeria, principally through preferential export taxes requiring that the ores be reduced in British plants, and through production and price agreements with the Dutch East Indies. The British government has taken an active interest in the nickel industry of Canada, in the manganese industry of the Gold Coast of Africa, and in the effort to secure high-grade iron ores abroad to supplement the low-grade domestic supplies.

Australia, the Union of South Africa, and Canada, and their constituent states and provinces, all exercise further measures of control. Australia puts restrictions on alien acquisition of minerals, and South Africa on all aliens other than white. All construe minerals as the property of the government to be extracted only under lease. The Union of South Africa restricts diamond output through a syndicate of principal producers cooperating with the government. It also is participating in the building up of an iron and steel industry. The Canadian government and some of its provincial governments have given special aid to the building

of refining and smelting establishments, have built
railways to mineral deposits and guaranteed bonds
on others, paid bounties on oil and iron ore, and
taken part in aiding Canadian and British capital to acquire control of the International Nickel
Company, formerly dominated by American capital.
In certain Canadian laws there are definite state-
ments regarding the necessity of refining the ores
produced within Canada. Indirect influence on
mineral development is exercised by political rela-
tionships to railways, which in turn have mineral
interests.

In general the Canadian, Australian, and South
African governments are doing all in their power to
make their mineral industries independent by building smelters, refineries, and factories, and thereby
to lessen the volume of outflowing raw minerals to
feed the industries of the United States, Great
Britain, and Europe. Protective tariffs are being
used as one of the aids to this movement. Recent
Australian tariffs are especially notable.

British capital plays a large part in the mineral
industries of the entire empire, and Great Britain
makes no secret of its desire to unify the group and
round it out by supplying deficiencies. As yet, however, this effort falls far short of complete commercial and political integration. The group is widely
scattered, with much autonomous political control,
as in Canada, Australia, and South Africa, and is

enmeshed in many ways with world industry outside of the British empire. It remains one of the
interesting questions for the future how far it can
be made to function as a single unit, and, if so, what
the relations of this unit will be to the other great
unit of the United States. On the solution of this
question largely depends the intelligent administration of minerals in the interest of world welfare and
peace.

The copper situation furnishes a good illustration
of this problem of unification of British control.
Heretofore Great Britain has been dependent upon
the United States for nearly all of its copper,
but great discoveries of copper in Rhodesia and
Canada promise independence if they can be
operated under British control. In both places there
has been keen commercial competition for control
between British and American interests, with mixed
results. Political factors were involved when control
of the International Nickel Company mines, containing large reserves of copper, was wrested from
American control. Also, there has been frank
discussion of the possibility of limiting American
voting rights in South African copper companies.
The goal is a counter combination to offset the
Copper Export Association controlled by American
interests. Some such counter combinations seem to
be a likely outcome. Whether the result will be intensified competition or cooperation remains to be seen.

NATIONAL POLICIES

France

All mineral resources of France and its colonies not already alienated are the property of the government, which has wide discretion in granting concessions. Alien ownership is prohibited. Under the San Remo agreement, British interests are allowed to participate in oil concessions in the French colonies and zones of influence up to 33 per cent, the remainder to be French (see pages 117–118).

The French government exploits the coal mines of the Saar and the potash deposits of Alsace, taken over from Germany. Germany and France between them have a world monopoly of potash. The Société Minerais et Metaux, organized under government auspices, takes considerable part in the lead, zinc, copper, and other industries. France is developing refining capacity by preferential duties rather than subsidy, although there is some direct subsidy, especially in connection with exploration in French North Africa.

Germany

All subsoil minerals are the property of the nation. Two states have rights to coal and salt. The Prussian government operated many coal mines before the war, but many of these are now under Poland's control. The potash industry is entirely under control of the German government. By agreement with the French government, which now controls the potash of Alsace, the potash market of the world is dominated. The German government has been especially active in the development of cartels and other similar aids to the advancement of German mineral industries, and has used its powers widely in coordinating and controlling nearly all phases of these industries, including transportation, tariffs, and subsidies. The German producers and fabricators of aluminum products are working toward a sliding tariff which will reserve the local market to the domestic industry.

Germany's position is a difficult one. Essential parts of her limited mineral supplies were taken away by the war settlement, the inflow of minerals from some sources was seriously impaired by new trade arrangements resulting from the war, and the opportunity of developing resources in the colonies was, of course, lost with the colonies. Political and commercial rapprochement with France and Poland, now under way, is the first and most obvious step to restore the efficiency of German mineral industries (see pages 62–63). The German government is attacking the problem with characteristic energy and thoroughness. It remains to be seen what success will be attained. Under the circumstances it is not surprising that the Germans favor the adoption of some international plan of administering natural resources as a means of insuring needed supplies from sources under the political and commercial control of other nations.

Russia

Under the present régime all minerals are nationalized. Some are operated directly by the state, others through concessions to commercial companies in which the government retains an interest. Especial efforts are being made to increase production in oil, coal, iron, manganese, copper, lead, and zinc, under the Five-year Plan. Results are already large. It is the boldest experiment in state operation of minerals anywhere under way.

Spain

Minerals are the property of the nation, and most of the well-known mineral districts are closed to prospecting. Under a decree of 1921, no mining concession may be issued to aliens, but treaty rights have delayed its application to nationals of Great Britain or Holland. The government monopolizes the production, importation, and sale of oil, expropriating, at its own terms, alien companies formerly engaged in this business. Also it retains complete control of potash, known to exist, but not yet mined in quantity. Together with Italy, Spain controls the production and sale of most of the world's mercury.

Italy

According to Italian law, the ownership of land does not convey rights to the resources of the subsoil, which are considered the property of the state, to be exploited only under official concession. The government has instituted a vigorous mineral policy with a double purpose: first, to make the country more nearly self-sufficient, and, second, to conserve the natural resources. This has resulted in an increase in the production of lead and zinc and a decrease for bauxite on account of the export restrictions. Under the auspices of the government, an Italian steel syndicate has been formed which embraces about 95 per cent of the country's capacity. Oil storage and refining plants have been increased beyond commercial requirements as a measure of national defense.

Latin-American Countries

In all Latin-American countries mineral developments have been almost exclusively in the hands of foreigners. In the past the governments granted a great deal of freedom to outside capital, but as mineral production has become established there has been a marked wave of legislation designed to further political control, as a defensive reaction against wholesale exploitation from without. Considerable impetus was given to this movement by the post-war flare of nationalism, based on the principle of self-determination of nations, so much discussed at the Peace Conference.

In nearly all Latin-American countries undiscovered minerals are now the property of the government. Concessions are given with far greater restrictions, both as to areas and terms, than was formerly the custom. In one way or another the effort is being made to eliminate foreign political influence from the control of concessions. In Colombia, Venezuela, and Argentina foreign governments are not allowed to obtain lease contracts or any interest in lease contracts. In Peru it is provided that any disagreement between the government and the concessionaire must be decided by local courts, without the intervention of foreign governments. In Mexico the new mining laws provide that only Mexicans and Mexican companies have the right to obtain mining concessions, and that the same right may be granted to foreigners only when they agree not to invoke the protection of their governments in matters pertaining to such concessions. Other decrees sought to substitute fifty-year concessions on oil lands for some of the more indefinitely drawn concessions of earlier date, and provided for the forfeiture of lands claimed for which concessions had not been applied for within one year. They also greatly limit the conditions under which mines may be developed and operated. In the hope of stimulating production, the Mexican government has also enacted a law providing for a sliding tax scale, to enable the local oil producers to meet outside competition.

In Chile the government has taken an active part in the nitrate industry, and a large part of the state revenue has come from the export tax on nitrates. Recently Chile has taken steps to nationalize the nitrate industry by combining all operations into a single large company, half of the stock to be owned by the government. Hereafter, the export tax will be eliminated, the government securing its revenue from the proceeds of the company. The adoption of this plan is largely due to the growing competition of synthetic nitrates which has materially impaired the monopoly of natural nitrates possessed by Chile. Under the initiative of the Chilean government price agreements have been made since the war by Chilean producers, and such agreements with German and British producers of synthetic nitrate are being worked out.

In Argentina the principal petroleum resources have been withdrawn from private ownership but may be operated by private interests under contract with the government. The government is directly engaged in exploration, production, and sale of oil. Peru has established a petroleum monopoly in accordance with the law which prohibits industrial and commercial monopolies and cartels, reserving for the state the rights to form such organizations.

In Brazil both the national government and the government of the Province of Minas Geraes have taken an active part in negotiating terms under which iron ores could be produced from the great reserves in Minas Geraes. In return for the privilege of exportation alien owners are to build a plant capable of supplying local needs for iron and steel.

Export taxes are widely used by South American countries. Notable cases are the export tariffs on nitrate from Chile, tin from Bolivia, vanadium from Peru, and oil from Venezuela and Mexico.

The detailed steps in the direction of strengthening public control in Latin-American countries are so many and varied that even the briefest mention of them all would make tedious reading. Enough illustrations have perhaps been given to indicate the general trend.

Needless to say, this political tendency has generally been opposed by alien commercial interests involved, which in many cases have had the strong support of their governments. Commercial interests of the United States have probably put on more pressure than those of any other nation, by virtue of the variety and extent of their holdings, but there has been little political pressure from our government. In Argentina, Costa Rica, and Mexico Americans have secured special rights to explore for oil by the application in the United States of the provisions of our Leasing Act, that foreigners should be excluded from the development of our public lands if we were excluded from theirs. Rights have also been acquired independently of the act in these countries and Venezuela. While it is often charged by Latin-American countries that the United States is using the Monroe Doctrine as a shield to protect its own activities, there is yet no case of mineral exploitation on the part of the United States in which the Monroe Doctrine has played any obvious part. Indirectly it may have been an influence against strong competing measures by European countries.

The Far East

For parts of the Far East under western political control the situation has been discussed or implied in connection with the political control of minerals for the British Empire, France, Russia, the Netherlands, and the United States. There remain to be discussed only Japan and China.

Japan.—Japan imposes restrictions which make it practically impossible for foreign companies to retain mining rights in the empire and none such exist. However, foreign mining companies conduct operations on a small scale in Korea and Manchuria. The Japanese government is directly associated in the operation of some of the mineral resources within its boundaries and in the oil industry of Formosa, China, and Sakhalin Island. Its largest and most obvious effort is the development, through the South Manchurian Railway, of the great coal seam and the oil shales of Fushun in Manchuria, and the iron ore of Anshan. It is active in mining iron ores in Formosa and Malay, and generally in the development of the Japanese iron and steel industry. In view of the shortage of mineral resources in the Japanese empire the success or failure of the Manchurian enterprises is a matter of considerable consequence to the Japanese nation. Japan also controls the output of the Hanyehping Iron and Coal Company, together with China's most available iron ore resources near Hankow on the Yangtze river, with the aid of a considerable amount of political pressure. This resource, it is to be remembered, figured in the famous twenty-one demands which Japan made of China in 1915. Due to the upset political condition in China, Japan is now unable to operate these deposits.

The Japanese government keenly realizes its lack of raw materials, and the acquirement of minerals is one of the cardinal features of its foreign policy. Its activities are much restricted by political obstacles thrown up by the great powers around their holdings in Asia, and by the political antipathy of China. Almost the only spot where Japan has a fairly free hand is in Manchuria.

China.—China restricts its mining rights to Chinese citizens or citizens of treaty power nations when doing joint business with Chinese, but under the condition that such foreign interest shall not exceed one-half. In practice it has been possible for alien interests to acquire minerals in China, and practically all the mineral industry is now in such hands. However, the new Chinese government gives every indication of taking over these interests as fast as commercial and political conditions will allow. Some of the provinces are also acting independently to accomplish the same results. The present chaotic conditions have retarded production, and for some time ahead there probably will not be any quickening of mining activity either by Chinese or by foreigners.

Résumé

The governments of all nations possessing minerals are taking an increasingly active political interest in the mineral industry. The nature of this interest varies with the different relations of the local industry to world conditions. All are attempting to foster domestic industries, and to retain minerals in their own regions of political control for their own nationals. Countries possessing insufficient minerals for large industrial development are trying to curb exploitation from without, in the effort to gain for themselves as large a benefit as possible from such minerals as they possess. The two nations which are most active in exploiting minerals outside of their own political spheres of influence are the United States and Great Britain. In both cases political aid is being given to this effort. This is especially true of the British government, but the United States government is showing increased activity. In the simplest possible terms, then, the situation resolves itself into competition between the British and American governments, with the rest of the nations of the world acting defensively against both.

Up to the present, the approach to the question of political control of minerals has been mainly along national lines. International understandings and agreements have mainly centered around the problem of the "open door." In a few cases they relate to production and marketing, as in the Franco-German potash agreement, the Spanish-Italian mercury agreement, and others. International commercial agreements not entered into directly by governments are far more numerous. The status of international control is more fully discussed in Chapter VIII.

Chapter V

THE NATURE OF SPECIFIC POLITICAL MEASURES

KEEPING in mind the main trends of the political policies of the nations in regard to minerals, we may to advantage inquire more closely into the nature and working of some of the more commonly applied political measures. Full detail is not available in the present stage of knowledge, but some of the main features are more or less obvious.

Import Tariffs

Import tariffs are imposed for various reasons, to protect an established mineral industry, to foster or create one, to furnish revenue. Import tariffs on smelted and finished products (together with export tariffs on raw materials, taxes, and patent laws) are often used to build up domestic smelting, refining, and manufacturing enterprises. In some cases there is conservational gain in smelting and manufacturing near the source of raw material supply, but in others there are opposing factors, market, geographic considerations, return cargoes, and the like, which make such procedure expensive and inefficient in that it tends to interfere with the natural channels of flow fixed by nature. As a means of stopping unification of world commercial control it has thus far proved ineffective.

In the United States, tariffs on minerals of which the domestic supply is inadequate, of low grade, or badly located, allow larger domestic production than would otherwise be possible. This is accomplished at higher cost to consumers, and often means also the use of inferior grades which without protection would not be used in preference to foreign supplies. To some extent, therefore, such tariffs tend to interfere with the normal flow of minerals from the world centers of production capable of affording the largest and cheapest supplies. While such interference is intended, in actual practice the tariff does more to raise cost than it does to reduce imports. Conditions of quality, uniformity of grade, and reliability of delivery insure the continued use of certain foreign minerals, especially in view of the fact that prices of domestic supplies rise with the tariff. The domestic producer benefits at the expense of the consumer, but, on the other hand, employment is increased, and the industry may be fostered to a really competing status if geologic conditions are right, or, even if they are not, the industry may be brought to a stage of development which would make it highly useful in case of war. There is,

[103]

of course, in this situation a wide field for controversy as to the political and commercial desirability of specific tariffs.

Where mineral exploration has yielded such prolific results as in the United States, it is not surprising that optimism should occasionally lead to efforts to accomplish the impossible by means of tariff. In this category manganese is one of several examples. The net effect of such tariffs in practice is to raise cost, without material reduction of imports, and to keep barely alive a few domestic operations struggling against highly adverse natural conditions. While this effort leads to the testing of all geologic and technologic possibilities and adds to our knowledge of potential supplies, at the same time it depletes the few domestic supplies available, which might to better advantage be conserved for times of national emergency when cost is a secondary consideration. It is a costly and, in the long run, a futile effort to create by enactment something which was not created by nature.

With mounting domestic demand the United States in the future will have to draw on foreign sources for increasing proportions of its minerals, particularly copper and oil, and the call for protection by domestic producers, already in evidence, is likely to be more insistent (see page 50).

What has been said of the United States has broad applications in other countries. Since the war there has been a multiplication of mineral import tariffs designed to create national units of industry. This has been especially true in Europe, where there has been a distinct attempt to dismember, by tariffs and other political measures, large international units of industry which before the war were either forming or actually functioning. The result has been to hinder free movements of minerals and to impair the European competitive position. Signs are not wanting, in suggestions of the League of Nations, the Economic Conference, the International Chamber of Commerce, and various special treaties, that some of the extreme phases of disintegration through tariffs are already in process of reversal. Preferential tariffs are steps in the direction of group protection and coordination, as illustrated by the British Empire.

Mineral import tariffs are inherently discriminatory against certain nations in their actual effect, even when they are not specifically differential or preferential. This arises from the fact that the sources of supply are so few. A tariff on manganese from whatever source comes down to a tariff on manganese from only five countries. Inequalities of economic opportunity and political friction are not uncommon results.

Export Tariffs[1]

The most notable case of export tariffs is the one on nitrate from Chile which in the past has supplied a large part of the total Chilean revenues. Other examples are tariffs on vanadium and copper from Peru, magnesite from Austria, graphite from Madagascar, lead, copper, and other ores from Spain, manganese from Brazil, diamonds from South Africa, bauxite from British Guiana, and all minerals from China. The British preferential export tax on Malay tin insures that it be treated in British plants. The same is true of Canadian asbestos. Minor export tariffs on minerals for revenue purposes are fairly widespread outside of the United States. This kind of tariff is unconstitutional in the United States.

The imposition of export tariffs has been for a great variety of reasons: revenue, conservation, restriction of output, control of markets and prices, to foster smelting, refining, and manufacturing industries at home, and others. They are borne by the purchaser only when they relate to a mineral under monopolistic control or with such advantages of situation and cost as will give it marked advantage over other competing sources. Where the

[1] IOANNOU, FLORENCE K., and ROBERTA P. WAKEFIELD, "Export Duties of the World," Foreign Tariff Series, No. 42, Bur. Foreign and Domestic Commerce, U. S. Dept. Commerce, Washington, D. C., 1927.

mineral is exported in competition with other countries, the price cannot be raised and the burden falls on the producer. The money collected, in some cases, is spent in whole or in part on the betterment of the industry.

The only export taxes of international concern are those which raise prices to the consumer. They stimulate the search for alternative sources and cause irritation and protest in the consuming countries. But looked at broadly, the international movement of minerals has been only slightly modified by export taxes. When these begin to cut down export they are likely to be modified to preserve volume of movement.

Bounties and Embargoes

Such measures have been not uncommon devices to stimulate domestic production and smelting of minerals which under normal conditions are not competitive either through lack of development or through adverse factors of quantity, distribution, and extraction costs. Here and there they have aided domestic production, as in the case of silver in the United States under the Pitman Act, but there seems to be no outstanding case of this kind where development by such means has been large enough to figure permanently in the world picture of production.

[107]

During the World War the United States restricted the importation of nearly all minerals, and completely prohibited that of iron ore, clay, and salt. Exports also were controlled. Similar embargoes and restrictions of imports and exports were commonly used by all belligerent countries. Restrictions persisted in some countries, and for some commodities, well beyond the war period, but at present there seems to be no outstanding case in any part of the world of marked interference with any major channel of mineral movement between countries.

Taxes

A review of mineral taxation discloses a highly chaotic and shifting situation which reflects a public awakening to the value of minerals in the national economy and to the fact that mineral deposits are wasting assets. In many parts of the world minerals are more heavily taxed than other forms of property, on the ground that they are a heritage of the people and they cannot be reproduced. Not only are they put on the tax roll at a higher rate or at higher value than other property, but they are subjected to many special supertaxes, licenses, and fees. Illustrations of this in the United States are the occupation and severance taxes on sulphur and oil in Louisiana and Texas, the occupation and royalty taxes on iron ores in Minnesota, severance taxes on minerals in Arkansas, the Montana tax on coal and oil, the anthracite tax of Pennsylvania. Measures of this kind come up perennially in various legislatures, and mining operators live in constant fear of additional taxes. It is not uncommon these days in the appointment of mine managers to consider political as well as technical ability. In the drawing of leases and the commercial valuation of mineral properties also this factor appears. In the adoption of such measures much is said of the special public interest, even though the measures themselves may not mention the motives. The Minnesota Tax Commission in its report of 1928 refers to legislative sentiment that iron ore, being a product of nature, is a natural heritage of the people, and states that the so-called "heritage and diminishing value" theories have played an important part in the legislative decision to differentiate in the basis of assessment as between iron ore and other property.[1]

Curiously enough our Federal income tax treats the wasting asset idea in quite a different way. Because minerals are wasting assets, considerable parts of earnings are regarded as distribution of capital and not taxable. Capital value must be established as on March 1, 1913, or through subsequent discovery, to the satisfaction of the government. Under this law owners of mineral property

[1] Eleventh Biennial Report, Minnesota Tax Commission, p. 131, 1928.

are invited to establish a capital value large enough to cover all known and potential reserves, whereas for purposes of local and state taxation acceptance of such values would lead to crushing tax burdens. The British income tax on minerals does not recognize the wasting-asset principle.

The present mounting taxation on certain United States minerals is speeding up the search for other supplies both at home and abroad, but the chances are that by the time these other supplies are largely in demand they also will have to carry an equivalent burden of taxation.

Government Participation in the Mineral Industry

There are increasing numbers of cases of direct commercial participation by governments in exploration, development, production, and marketing of mineral products, both in domestic and in foreign fields. "Economic penetration" is often closely linked with imperialistic aims. In many cases it is impossible to separate the commercial and political interests involved. Illustrative of this are the participation of the British government in the Anglo-Persian Oil Company, the Turkish Petroleum Company, the British South African Company, and the International Nickel Company (through original stock ownership in the British American Nickel Company, which later was absorbed by the Mond Nickel Company and then by International Nickel), the Japanese operations in coal and iron in Manchuria, the Russian government operations in all minerals, the Argentine government's activity in oil exploration and production, the German control of the potash industry and maintenance of the coal syndicate, and many others. A special feature of the French mining law is the compulsory participation of the personnel in the profits of the mining enterprise, along with the government, after the concessionaire has been allowed a certain percentage. A similar law exists in Turkey. Public financial aid is becoming an effective means of mineral development in places which do not attract private capital, or for purposes of stronger competition with outside sources, or as a means of exclusion of outside capital.

Much political attention is being focused on the smelting, mining, and manufacturing of domestic minerals in the effort to keep a larger portion of the profit at home. In many parts of the world governments are fostering domestic smelting and manufacturing by direct financial aid, operation, guaranteeing of bonds, special transportation rates, tariffs, and bounties. In this category comes the activity of the Canadian and provincial governments in encouraging the building of smelters at Trail, at Sudbury, and in the Rouyn district.

Governments in many parts of the world have been active in building railways into mineral districts, in guaranteeing the bonds of such railways, or in controlling railways giving special rate concessions favoring domestic production. Canada, again, furnishes several illustrations of this kind, in the building of railways to new mineral deposits in Manitoba, to the Cobalt, Porcupine, and other districts of Ontario, and to the Rouyn district of Quebec. In fact there has hardly been a major mineral discovery in the past thirty years in which local or state governments have not been interested in one way or another in the problem of transportation.

Political Control of Associations, Cartels, Institutes, Syndicates

The drawing together of the separate units of the mineral industry into associations of one kind or another for the purpose of controlling production, prices, or markets has been a notable feature of the mineral industry, as already indicated. Nations or state governments have aided in the organization, provided or modified laws to make them possible, and in some cases even forced the industries to adhere to the combinations. Illustrative of such political encouragement is the part played by the Chilean government in the Nitrate Association, the passage of the Webb Act by the United States as a means of allowing collective selling abroad, the activities of the Oil Conservation Board of the United States, the application of the "Rule of Reason" to the Sherman Act, and the establishment in

France and Germany of associations to control the production and marketing of potash.

On the other hand, the general policy in the United States has been opposed to such combinations and is reflected in the Sherman Act, the Wilson Tariff Act and its amendment, the Panama Canal Law, the Clayton Act, and the Federal Trade Commission Act, to prevent their establishment. At the present moment the unification of control of minerals in the United States is undoubtedly being held back by fear of legal action. In view of the world-wide tendency in this field, which seems to be securely based on the physical requirements of the situation, it is clear that the United States must again review and decide the political question of how far these combinations will be allowed to go in the direction of unit control of the industry.

The English policy has also been to restrict monopolies or combinations and preserve free competition in the interest of the consumer and of the small producer and trader, but a more sympathetic attitude toward industrial agreements has been noted in recent years.

Nationalization of Mineral Resources

Nearly all of the measures previously referred to are in the nature of nationalization of mineral resources, in the sense of closer government control, but there are, in addition, many measures of nationalization in the narrower sense of the direct acquirement by the nation of mineral ownership and operation. Most of the nations of the world now declare minerals in the public domain the property of the government, to be leased or operated by private interests only under restrictions and payment of rentals and royalties to the government. Even the United States has now done this under the Leasing Act for its remaining public domain for coal, petroleum, gas, and a number of other minerals. Many nations have gone farther and have claimed the ownership of undiscovered minerals in lands which have passed into private ownership. It is not uncommon in the Latin-American countries to distinguish between surface and sub-surface minerals, the former going to the owner of the land, and the latter to the government. In some cases even the owner of the surface has no preferential right whatever to minerals which may be found below the surface. Finally there are the extreme cases of actual dispossession of private owners by the government and complete state control and operation, as in Russia.[1] Usually these measures are applied only to certain minerals of sub-surface kind, but in a few cases they apply to all minerals.[2]

[1] Russia has also renounced all claims to concessions acquired by the former government in Persia and agreed to do the same in China.

[2] The interested reader may now find this information in convenient form in a series of Information Circulars published by the U. S. Bureau of Mines summarizing the mining laws of all countries.

The present world-wide trend toward nationalization is not entirely new in history, though it has taken on new aspects. In the early small beginnings of the use of minerals it was the rule rather than the exception for the crown to retain ownership of precious metals and stones, and later even of iron, copper, and other metals essential to military preparation. This is true of all the countries of Europe. Later this control became more or less separated from the crown in some countries by dispersion through the noble classes or by leases and concessions. Only in England was this carried through to a stage of complete private ownership, and this principle was later the dominant one governing the disposition of mineral resources in all English-speaking countries. The major separation of minerals from state control went on during the period of the industrial revolution. At the same time many countries, particularly in Europe, never departed from the earlier form of control.

International Measures

The Closed Door.—Under this heading are included a vast range of measures designed to restrict foreign participation in the domestic mineral industry. Some of the restrictions are complete, some are incomplete, some are direct and some are indirect. Some apply only to certain minerals, others apply only to certain aliens, still others are designed to restrict the marketing activities of foreign monopolies. In fact there are about as many different ways of exclusion as there are countries. Further, there is such a rapid change in measures, and in their interpretation and enforcement, that it is almost impossible, with the present facilities for collecting information, for any one to keep fully up to date with the status of the "closed door" in all parts of the world. In general it may be said that there is almost no mineral-bearing country in the world that does not exercise some degree of restriction on alien participation. At one extreme stand the United States and Canada with restrictions which are very limited in their application; at the other are France, Russia, and Japan, in which any alien activity in mineral resources is exceptional and under special arrangement with the government.

Some of the more direct exclusion acts have been mentioned in Chapter IV. Indirect methods are often fully as effective in accomplishing the desired result. For instance, several countries, notably Spain and Japan, provide for alien participation where such is approved by certain government officials, but such approval is difficult to secure. There are countries where the laws provide for alien participation but where participation in practice is effectively prevented by dilatory tactics designed to wear out the applicant.

Under these circumstances exploitation by foreign interests is falling more and more into the hands of powerful companies able to exert pressure and make special bargains with the government, or is being confined to the nationals of those countries which are sufficiently powerful politically to secure these rights for their nationals. As the principal exploiting countries of the world are the United States and Great Britain, both of which are powerful politically and commercially, it is not surprising that the closed-door barriers of the world have often been successfully surmounted or circumvented by the nationals of these countries. Our strong American oil companies not only have done well by themselves, but have received powerful aid in certain countries by the invocation on the part of our government of the reciprocal clause in our Leasing Act.

The question of the open and closed door was brought into the limelight by the agreement between the British and French governments at San Remo in 1920, in regard to petroleum interests in Rumania, Old Russia, Asia Minor, Mesopotamia, the French colonies of North Africa, and the colonies of the British crown. This accorded mutual rights and concessions in the territories of the two groups, equal division of concessions and rights acquired in former enemy concessions, and the joint support of the two governments to their nationals for their common efforts in Russia. This immediately lead to protest by the United States and other governments. One of the direct results was to secure participation in the Mesopotamian operations for American oil companies to an extent of 25 per cent, the same proportion as had been allowed to France. It was also agreed that this company should be under the permanent control of Great Britain. The orderly exploration and development of the Mesopotamian fields (now through a subsidiary company called the Iraq Petroleum Company) has been an outstanding example of international development of the resources of a backward nation to the mutual advantage of all concerned, including Iraq.[1]

It is becoming more and more difficult for commercial companies alone to secure the necessary concessions, and thus it is that governments figure ever more prominently in this effort to open the door for mineral development. As the door is also closed by governments, it follows that the question where mineral development shall go on, and by what agencies, is, in fact, largely an international political problem, and will become increasingly so in the future. The time has gone by when the individual prospector with small capital can go

[1] For detailed account of these activities see HORNBECK, STANLEY K., "The Struggle for Petroleum," *Ann. Am. Acad. Polit. and Soc. Sci.*, No. 201, pp. 162–171, March, 1924.

freely about the world on his own resources to find minerals.

Concessions.—Closely related to the open-door problem is the subject of foreign concessions. Here is abundant material awaiting the investigator which has not yet been studied in any comprehensive way.

Concessions and grants for the purpose of exploration and development take on a very wide variety of forms and range all the way from permits to exploit individual claims, to nation-wide concessions. They vary from nation to nation, from mineral to mineral, and from time to time. Many special bargains with individual commercial interests and nations are included. They serve to give the government revenue and some control of the industry. When granted by a weaker nation to strong foreign interests they have been a frequent source of political difficulty, so much so in fact that in recent years new concessions have nearly all contained a provision that the concessionaire should have the right to appeal only to the local courts and not to the home government.

During the early exploration stage, and particularly in the case of petroleum, there seem to be necessity and economic justification for concessions covering large areas in order to induce and justify the expenditures necessary for careful exploration work in new regions. Where such concessions are safeguarded by the stipulation that within a limited period of, say, three to five years, the holder must select for retention a small percentage of the original exploration area, the result is development without exclusion. Exclusive concessions on large areas without such a reduction factor are economically unsound (see page 179).

Many of the earlier concessions in backward nations were loosely and vaguely drawn, for too long a time and too great areas, without adequate safeguards to the nation. There was too much twilight zone of controversy. The history of the troubles in working out the Chester concessions in Turkey, the Turkish petroleum concessions in Mesopotamia, and the Mexican oil concessions, is typical of many concessions. Since the war many nations have made a determined effort to revise these concessions, and particularly to define them more precisely as to both time and area, and to recover to some extent national rights which had been carelessly alienated. This effort has in some cases had the support of the concessionaires themselves on the ground that a bargain needs to be fair if it is to have permanent validity. The government of Colombia appointed an outside commission of engineers to advise in regard to revision of its oil concessions, and the recommendations of this board embody valuable suggestions for future concessions based on principles which have been found to be workable and fair. In this field, as in others, there are good methods and bad methods. Here is a wide opportunity for the mining profession to aid in the elimination of bad methods in the interest of international welfare and peace.

Treaties, Conventions, Agreements.—The rights to engage in mining are referred to in a great many treaties; either specifically, or by inference under general clauses, such as are present universally in the bilateral commercial treaties that are in force between almost all nations. These articles are to the effect that each contracting party will extend to the nationals of the other party all the rights accorded to its own nationals, subject to the local laws and regulations. These clauses are actually of little importance, as the tendency toward the "closed door" in nearly all countries is reflected in the domestic laws, which are either highly restrictive or completely exclusive to foreigners who wish to develop natural resources.

The treaties which make specific mention of mining rights are too numerous to list here. A few of the articles are prohibitive in nature, others grant all mining rights, and some restrict the rights to certain minerals. As illustrations, it may serve to mention the conventions concerning mandated territories which grant mining concessions to the nationals of most countries, and the recent United States commercial treaties which allow mining of certain minerals by the nationals of each contracting party. The multilateral treaty, signed by the principal powers, which establishes the conditions governing mining in Spitsbergen is not a common type of agreement, and the famous San Remo Agreement between France and Great Britain is another example of a document to cover a special case.

The flow of minerals and mineral products is controlled to some extent by commercial treaties, containing either general or detailed customs regulations.

Agreements relating to production and marketing are illustrated by the Franco-German control of potash, the Spanish-Italian control of mercury, the British-Dutch control of tin smelting through preferential tariffs, and the Japanese-Chinese agreement about the Yangtze iron industry. Doubtless there are many others. Trade journals and newspapers have reported many understandings and negotiations among the European nations. Changes are rapid and the data have not been assembled, but it is clear that measures of this kind are multiplying. The United States has not yet figured in international agreements of this kind, though the field has been here and there touched in connection with the open door and concessions.

Also to be mentioned under this heading are some of the recommendations of the World Economic Conference and the League of Nations discussed in Chapter VIII.

SPECIFIC POLITICAL MEASURES

The Scope and Effectiveness of Political Measures

The present trend of political enactment is clearly in the direction of an adaptation of political background to commercial trends in the mineral industry, which are, in turn, determined in their main outlines by nature's distribution of raw materials. The great multiplication of specific measures in recent years is, in itself, a broad indication of the extent to which the operation and control of mineral resources is becoming a political as well as a commercial problem. The approach has been mainly along national lines, though international measures are on the increase.

The national measures have secured material advantages in some countries. The more they are studied, the clearer it becomes that in actual practice they have modified, but not radically changed, the flow of minerals and the commercial trends in the industry.

It is also clear that while some national measures are wisely thought out and locally helpful, many others reflect merely a national hope or ambition for self-sufficiency, economic equality, and self-determination, without full consideration of world conditions. Some of these measures have already been proved by experience to be uneconomic and futile, and others are likely to be so proved in the future. With the partial and chaotic information

[123]

heretofore available it is not surprising that legis-
lators and officials have made mistakes in their
laudable ambition to do the best for their countries.
On the one side they have had specific local information and pressure, on the other only vague and
often conflicting information. There is now opportunity for effective political achievement by taking
advantage of the rapidly clearing perspective of
the world mineral situation.

International measures have mainly touched the
question of the open door and concessions, with a
few relating to production and marketing. None of
them covers all nations and most of them are limited
to a few. Some of them have been designed to aid
and define commercial trends based on nature's distribution of minerals, others have been designed to
change them. None of them has resulted in radical
changes which promise to be permanent. As in
national approach, mistakes have been made and
political readjustments are following the commercial
trends.

Chapter VI

CONSERVATION[1]

MANY of the richer mineral deposits and districts have been exhausted or are on the decline, and the trend is toward the utilization of lower-grade supplies (see Chapter II). When all the low-grade and high-cost deposits are taken into account, world supplies are ample for a very long time, with the possible exception of gold and oil. Price is an important factor in determining how much mineral is available. The best and most available of the world's minerals, however, are being rapidly depleted. The situation is well illustrated by coal, the total reserves of which are so huge as to cause no worry for the future, but when the situation is analyzed it appears that the higher-grade coals conveniently located for exploitation have very definite limitations.

[1] ELY, RICHARD T., RALPH H. HESS, CHARLES K. LEITH, and THOMAS NIXON CARVER, "The Foundations of National Prosperity," The Macmillan Company, New York, 1917.

"Conservation of Our Natural Resources," based on Van Hise's "The Conservation of Natural Resources in the United States," edited by Loomis Havemeyer, The Macmillan Company, New York, 1930.

The growth of the idea of conservation has resulted from the rapidly expanding demands on mineral reserves, the exhaustion or rapid depletion of the best of them, the knowledge that even the largest of the remaining reserves will not last indefinitely. on the modern scale of production, the realization that mineral reserves are irreplaceable, and, finally, a better understanding of the fundamental necessity of minerals to modern industry and to national and economic welfare. There have been enough cases of wasteful exploitation to lend color to the popular belief that all exploitation has been of this kind. Indeed it is more or less the vogue to refer to our modern use of minerals as extravagant and wasteful, particularly in the United States, and to ascribe our present advancement to an unwarranted and extravagant use of nature's bounties.

The conservational problem includes consideration of the question how far production of key minerals of limited supply should be held back in peace times in favor of foreign importation, for the sake of having an emergency reserve for war (see page 104).

While the central idea of conservation has mainly related to possible shortage of material supplies, and this is yet the popular concept, it is coming to include another important consideration, namely, the conservation of human energy involved in winning the raw materials. This idea is largely embodied in the word "efficiency." The immediate problem for many of the mineral industries, which will last for many years, is the efficient handling of surplus of raw materials rather than deficiency. Does it pay to save a dollar's worth of mineral with the expenditure of two dollars' worth of human energy? For some minerals the supply is so small and precious that it may pay to spend large amounts in human effort to save the mineral. For others the supply is so abundant that large expenditure to save the mineral would be wasteful of the other conservational element—human energy. The charge that Americans are always wasteful of their raw materials fails to take into account the frequent saving in human effort. The careful saving of materials in Europe is equally open to the charge that it sometimes involves unnecessary waste of human labor. Which is to the best interest of society—the conservation of irreplaceable raw materials or replaceable human energy?

Still another general question is yet to be answered: whether the present use of minerals, even to the point of exhaustion, may not be more conducive to the progress of the race than holding back this use in the interest of posterity. Wasteful practice seems to be an almost inevitable accompaniment of the early stage of any mineral industry, due to lack of knowledge or financial support, but almost always the curve of efficiency rises, waste is eliminated, and a way is found to use progressively lower and lower grades of raw materials. Also for many minerals, such as copper, there is a large recovery of scrap which can be used again. To this extent the rapid extraction of minerals from the earth does not reduce their quantity and availability. Looking at the situation broadly, may it not be that our present impetuous attack on mineral reserves is but the necessary first step in a long orderly approach to the use of earth materials. A few resources of limited quantity may be seriously impaired by this initial attack, notably oil, but for much the greater part of the mineral resources now used industrially, the supply, known and potential, high and low grade, promises an indefinitely long future.

The call for some sort of public conservational action is based on the underlying assumption that this cannot be left to private initiative, which would be influenced only by selfish motives, and that public action alone can bring the desired results—a doubtful assumption which warrants careful examination. Conservation planks, like deep waterways, are common to nearly all political platforms in the United States. In one extreme case in recent years a platform included a demand for the "permanent conservation" of minerals, whatever that might mean. The platform did not explain.

CONSERVATION

In many countries conservation has been a popular slogan for the enactment not only of direct anti-waste measures but for closed-door legislation, tariffs, government aid to the integration of the mineral industry, and various measures designed to nationalize minerals.

Actual public enactments of a conservational nature have thus far been few in the United States. Withdrawals of minerals in the public domain have been essentially conservational measures in that they introduce much more rigid supervision of the manner and speed of extraction of minerals from the public domain. The United States Coal Commission appointed in 1922 and the Federal Oil Conservation Board appointed in 1924 have made valuable suggestions and have been helpful in aiding the mineral industry in conservational steps. State governments have cooperated with the industry in the attempt to stop overproduction of oil and gas. Import tariffs, resulting in higher selling prices, have permitted better mining practices in some instances.

Notwithstanding popular belief to the contrary, the mineral industry itself desires conservation as much as the public. To the industry it means higher efficiency, and in the long run larger returns; it means curtailment of production, lessening of ruinous competition, better labor conditions, and higher prices. There is a strong commercial incentive to proceed as far as possible along these lines, but leaders are not wanting who are in addition genuinely interested in running their industries along lines best in accord with public welfare. In fact, an impartial review of conservational measures which have been put into effect shows that by far the more numerous and effective ones have been initiated by the industry itself in its striving for higher efficiency. Standards of good mining require the cleanest possible extraction of ore. Much ingenuity and effort are expended to use as much as possible of ores which are badly located or of inferior grade. Even though operators may sometimes be tempted to leave such ores in the ground, they are prevented from doing so by vigilant fee owners whose interest is to secure the most value from the mineral deposits. Where commercial conditions do not allow the use of inferior grades at a profit, efforts are made to leave such parts of the deposit in such condition as will allow mining later, or if they have to be moved, that they are stockpiled for possible future use. No oil company willingly overproduces oil, or leaves 50 per cent or more of the oil in the ground when by the application of known technical methods this percentage can be reduced without eliminating profit. An immense range of new technical devices has come into use which makes possible recoveries not thought of a few years ago. The best technical brains are constántly striving to extend these processes, and the premiums for success are large.

Many notable advances in conservational practice have been made possible by the growth in size and financial strength of the commercial units of the industry. Also the growing dependence on the largest mineral reserves carries certain conservational advantages, in that the scale of operation allows of methods and refinements not possible in small deposits. During the war a study of copper production in the United States brought out in striking fashion the higher efficiency of the larger operations. It was found that the transfer of labor from some of the small marginal copper enterprises to the larger ones resulted in multiplying the output per man by as much as ten. This factor was taken into account in the government's issuance of priority orders for equipment and transportation. With a larger organization it is easier, even imperative, to take the long-range view, to introduce practices which will in the long run bring a better return from the resources as a whole, and to sacrifice some immediate larger return for the sake of major advantages for the future. This has made it possible to treat some mineral reserves as units, and to plan operations with a minimum capital charge designed to secure maximum returns from the reserve as a whole, rather than a piecemeal competitive attack by units too small to be able to control all of the conditions. The advantage of this is especially noticeable in oil pools where unit operation shows a great conservational gain over the necessarily wasteful practice resulting from divided ownership. Small, insecurely financed companies in a highly competitive field often find it necessary to extract only the highest-grade minerals by the cheapest, and perhaps wasteful, methods for the sake of immediate profit.

Even where unit commercial control is not possible, somewhat the same results can be obtained by agreement and understanding among the companies. It is obviously easier for a few strong companies to reach such agreements and to carry them through, than for a large number of small companies, some of which are handicapped by financial conditions, to carry through their agreements. Such small companies have often prevented the success of curtailment programs designed to secure better prices and more orderly and conservational practices of mineral extraction.

Unit control may even be international in scope. The orderly development of the oil resources of Iraq (Mesopotamia) through an international company, the Turkish Petroleum Company, and now the Iraq Petroleum Company, stands out in marked contrast to the disorderly and wasteful exploitation of the Venezuelan and Mexican oil arising from unrestricted competition of British and American oil companies. In Venezuela understandings among these companies are already beginning to ameliorate the situation.

Another great gain to be derived from cooperation or unification is the elimination of wasteful duplication in transportation and distribution. Unnecessary hauls are numerous throughout the list of commercial minerals. During the war, when economy of transportation was essential, much of this useless duplication was eliminated, but it has since come back as a consequence of competition. Conservation requires that, in general, consumption should draw upon the nearest adequate source of supply regardless of ownership or political control.

The establishment of research departments and research projects is a normal corollary of increasin size. The mining industry as a whole has lagged somewhat behind other industries in this activity, but at the present time is pushing ahead vigorously. The purpose of these investigations is essentially conservational even though they are not designated by this word.

Some of the main obstacles to further wide expansion of conservational practice, by the industry itself, are political. So far as Federal and state anti-trust laws prevent combinations they are anti-conservational in effect, whatever their other merits may be, in that they hinder rationalized control of production. Heavy special taxation of some minerals is also an anti-conservational influence. Minnesota iron ore taxes have now become so high that only the best and most favorably located of the open-pit deposits can be mined to the best advantage. Lower grade and underground ores of higher cost, which ought to be currently mined along with the lower cost ores, are in many cases left untouched. As the Mesabi range approaches exhaustion there will be a rapid increase in cost to recover these ores. The aggregate cost of recovery of Mesabi ore will be higher and the total efficiency lower because of excessive tax burden.

Probably the most effective bars to conservational practices are overproduction and low selling prices due to highly competitive conditions. There are immense quantities of natural gas, oil, and metallic minerals being wasted today because the cost of recovery would be beyond the selling price. Low price makes possible the use of oil for fuel, in place of coal which exists in vastly larger quantities, and, therefore, is highly wasteful of a relatively limited resource which can be refined to products of higher value.

Popular belief to the contrary, the profit or social surplus in the extraction of minerals from the earth, is not larger than in most other lines of industry, when account is taken of all the expenditures and failures in exploration and development. Unit control, either commercial or political, preventing overproduction, seems to be the only feasible way of maintaining prices on a sufficiently high and uniform standard to allow recovery of much of the minerals now being wasted. This situation has been clearly and concisely stated by various leaders of the mineral industry and by public commissions, but of course there is strong political objection due to the fear that monopoly powers will be misused, and that higher prices, while allowing of more conservation, will also allow excessive profits. It is said that when the view that the principal limit to conservation was the low selling price of oil was presented to a former President of the United States, he remarked dryly, "Yes, but I would not care to be running for office on such an issue."

One of the great political problems for the future will be to find some way to curb excessive profits arising from monopoly or unified control, but at the same time to allow selling prices which will permit urgently needed conservation. Can this be left to the industry itself, or is government or state control necessary? The question is both national and international in its scope.

The emergence of this central question can be clearly traced in the history of the conservational steps which have been taken by our Federal and state governments. The conservational movement, so-called, was really started in this country when President Roosevelt in 1908 formed a Conservation Commission, and called in the governors of the states and others for a conference. A considerable number of reports resulted directly and indirectly from this step, but the subject remained more or less in the field of academic discussion until the appointment of the United States Coal Commission in 1922 and of the Federal Oil Conservation Board in 1924. In several reports of these boards emphasis is placed on the necessity for integration of the industry under public supervision, and both boards have been active in their efforts to bring this about with the cooperation of state governments and industry. The Oil Conservation Board even went so far as to invite consultations looking toward international unification. These efforts, however, were definitely limited by the anti-trust laws. There followed, naturally, recommendations for the modification of the anti-trust laws, which have thus far not been acted upon. However, an amendment (1930) to the General Leasing Act permits lessees of government land to participate in unit operation of oil fields. The plan recognizes the oil pool in its sub-surface formation as the unit in development rather than the individual oil lease or tract of land.

Holders of separate tracts or leases, under this plan of development and operation, receive a proportionate interest in the area as a whole, with expenses and receipts divided proportionately. The states have been encouraged to use to the limit their police powers to prevent overproduction and waste. The states of California, Oklahoma, and Texas have made special efforts of this kind, which, while partially successful, are still regarded doubtfully as a means of permanent control. There is agreement among all concerned, the oil and coal commissions, the states, and the industries, that the integration of the industry must somehow be accomplished, preferably by the industry itself under public supervision, but the doubtful success of this program to date has raised the question whether the industry can become sufficiently integrated, even with the removal of anti-trust barriers, to accomplish the desired result. Most of the leaders of the mineral industry think it is possible, under general government supervision; others believe that it can be accomplished only by more or less direct control of the government.

In the meantime there is much room for the continued and expanding activity of Federal and state agencies in the study and initiation of conservational practices, in requiring the use of the best of them and particularly in encouraging cooperative efforts within the industry. There is a present need in the United States of a comprehensive study of conservational practice and theory—technical, commercial, and political—in other countries. There are, doubtless, lessons to be learned in the experience of European countries, such as Germany, which have given serious attention to this question for a long time.

Chapter VII

MINERALS AND WAR

Minerals in the Prosecution of War

THE Great War demonstrated the vital dependence of industrial and military power of the
nations on minerals. It was suddenly realized that
minerals were not everywhere available in adequate
amounts. Acquirement and protection of the few
adequate sources and transportation channels
became matters of vital military importance. The
blockade of the Central Powers in regard to copper,
manganese, nitrate, nickel, and many other minerals
deficient within their boundaries was a considerable
factor in the ultimate defeat of these powers. On the
other hand, the allies felt the lack of a few minerals,
particularly potash, available only in enemy territory, and the German occupation of the Lorraine
iron ore fields was a vital influence on the conduct
of the war. It was soon found necessary to establish
international committees for the allocation of certain
minerals and elimination of unnecessary ocean hauls.
Special national agencies were set up to develop
local supplies wherever possible, and thus to lessen

dependence on foreign sources and save ships for other military purposes. The impetus of this movement for local development in the United States is still reflected in some of the mineral fields like manganese, tungsten, and potash. For the first time nations learned something about the world mineral situation and particularly about their own deficiencies.

Since the war these problems have come to play a prominent rôle in the studies and plans of military staffs.[1] Attention centers on so-called "key" minerals (as well as other raw materials), that is, minerals essential to the prosecution of war which at the same time are so distributed as to present problems of acquirement in adequate amounts. Among the key minerals are practically the entire list of ferro-alloy minerals necessary for the manufacture of iron and steel; also tin, nickel, graphite, manganese, mica, and natural nitrates, nearly all of which are produced dominantly in countries far removed from countries of consumption. It is necessary to know all possible sources, both now producing and potential. In planning for the necessary war-time supplies of such minerals the major industrial nations face the prob-

[1] The importance of minerals from a military viewpoint is shown in the Armaments Year Book, an official publication of the League of Nations which, in addition to military and naval information, includes tables of production, importation, and exportation for coal, pyrites, manganese, tungsten, lignite, petroleum, iron, lead, zinc, copper, aluminum, nickel, sulphur, phosphates, nitrates, and salt.

lem of maintaining the channels of flow against various possible combinations of nations, keeping track of all commercial stocks in storage and in transit so that they may be commandeered in time of war, and building up extensive stocks specifically for war purposes. The last named method is the surest protection and may be said to be in general the desired goal of army and navy staffs the world over. The difficulty is, however, that stocks large enough to be really effective involve large investments, and it is difficult in peace times for many of the nations to secure public approval for this kind of preparation. In the United States, for instance, it seems clear that any adequate preparation for war will involve the storage of enough manganese for at least a year, but it is apparently easier for legislative bodies to vote for guns and ships than for less understood requirements in raw materials.

Among the surest criteria for judging preparedness for war are stocks of key minerals accumulated by governments in excess of commercial requirements. Since the war France has acquired reserves of manganese and other minerals considerably in excess of her commercial requirements, presumably as a step in preparedness. Italy has stored large quantities of oil, and built refining plants, apparently beyond commercial requirements. Unfortunately, such information is not easily obtainable. Publicity of such figures would go far toward focusing world attention on danger spots. This is strikingly illustrated by the German importation of key minerals immediately preceding the Great War, as indicated in the chart on page 143.

At the time these figures were not generally known, but interpretation of the figures in the light of what happened shows how clearly they pointed to danger ahead. In the first six months of 1914 Germany accumulated stocks of manganese, brass, nickel, tin, aluminum, asbestos, sulphur, graphite, and mica so far in excess of previous rates as to show beyond question that some extraordinary use was planned.

Any nation may start a war, but capacity to sustain it effectively under modern conditions is about commensurate with its industrial power based on minerals, particularly the mineral fuels, iron, copper, lead, and zinc. The time has gone by when military strength can be measured mainly by the number of men available. The hordes of Asia would break against the weapons of modern industrialism. From this point of view, therefore, the relative military strength of nations may be roughly inferred from the survey of mineral conditions given in Chapter III, where it is indicated that the seat of industrial power is likely to remain in North Atlantic countries for an indefinite future. No combination of nations in the rest of the world can marshal anywhere near the industrial power

MINERALS AND WAR

GERMANY'S PREPARATION FOR WAR
PRE WAR IMPORTS OF CERTAIN SELECTED MINERALS
NEEDED FOR MUNITION PURPOSES OF WHICH DOMESTIC
PRODUCTION IS INADEQUATE

The light line crossing each diagram diagonally indicates
the trend of German imports as a whole which increased
about 7 percent per year between 1910 and 1914.
Figures compiled by F.F. Grout (office of C.K.Leith)

MANGANESE ORE
TOTAL GERMAN IMPORTS
Data from "Mineral Indus-
try" for years 1909-1913 incl.
and from Gluckout vol.50 -
pt.X-6 mos. of 1914 -for esti-
mate for year 1914.
Figures in tons.
NOTE: Dotted line
indicates the
fluctuations in
steel industry.

1909 1910 1911 1912 1913 1914
Calendar Years

NICKEL
UNITED STATES TO GERMANY
Data from Foreign Commerce
and Navigation of the United
States.
Figures in pounds.

1910 1911 1912 1913 1914
Fiscal Years

TIN
STRAITS SETTLEMENTS
TO GERMANY, ETC.
Data from United
States Consular
Reports.
Figures in tons.

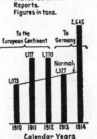

1910 1911 1912 1913 1914
Calendar Years

BRASS-ALL CRUDE FORMS
UNITED STATES TO GERMANY
Data from Foreign Commerce
and Navigation of
the United States.
Figures in Dollars.

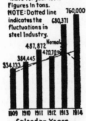

1910 1911 1912 1913 1914
Fiscal Years

ALUMINUM-& M'F'GS OF
UNITED STATES TO GERMANY
Data from Foreign Commerce
and Navigation of
the United States.
Figures in Dollars.

1910 1911 1912 1913 1914
Fiscal Years

ASBESTOS-CRUDE
CANADA TO GERMANY
Data from Canadian
Dept. of Mines.
Mines Br. Ann. Rep. 1918
p. 178.
Figures in tons.

1910 1911 1912 1913 1914
Calendar Years

SULPHUR
UNITED STATES TO GERMANY
Data from Foreign Commerce
and Navigation of
the United States.
Figures in tons.

1910 1911 1912 1913 1914
Fiscal Years

AM. COM. TO NEG. PEACE
Dvs. of Econ. and Stat.
Feb. 6, 1919.

GRAPHITE
UNITED STATES TO GERMANY
Data from Foreign Commerce
and Navigation of the United
States.
Figures in pounds.

1910 1911 1912 1913 1914
Fiscal Years

MICA
UNITED STATES TO GERMANY
Data from Foreign Commerce
and Navigation of the United
States.
Figures in Dollars.

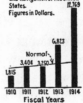

1910 1911 1912 1913 1914
Fiscal Years

of these nations because of the absence of the necessary raw materials. Even though deficient minerals may be freely imported, it is almost impossible for any country in emergency to build all the vast network of industrial plants necessary to convert the raw materials. This has to be done commercially under normal conditions, and requires a long time. The possibilities of emergency building are usually overestimated, because the necessary scale and time are underestimated.

Especially noteworthy is the fundamental lack of necessary raw materials in Asia, the Mediterranean, South America, and for the present in Germany.

Difficulties are encountered in appraising the mineral strength of the British Empire for war purposes because of the wide geographic scattering of its minerals, and the doubt about the extent to which they might be mobilized with unit control under the various potential alignments of enemy nations. To some extent this doubt extends to any minerals controlled politically and commercially by distant nations.

Minerals as Causes of War

International rivalries for the control of minerals have grown with increased mineral consumption, and with the realization that adequate sources are few and irreplaceable. They have naturally centered around key minerals most important to

industry and to national defense, or most limited
in quantity and in geographic distribution. While
mainly commercial and not in the public eye, these
rivalries are none the less determined and persistent.
From time to time there are signs of political
irritation and friction of a kind contributory to war.
The great growth of German metallurgical enterprises was a contributory cause of the commercial
jealousy which played its part in the development
of the Great War. Efforts toward territorial expansion have often been influenced by the desire to
secure potentially mineralized areas. Cases in
point are the German efforts to secure iron ore in
Morocco before the war, the British effort to secure
additional territory in Venezuela during the Cleveland administration, and boundary disputes between Chile and Peru. Much political friction was
created in Europe by the redistribution of territories
under the Peace Treaty which deprived some
nations of much needed raw materials. Austria
was almost stripped of its mineral deposits, and
Germany lost important mineral districts both in
the east and the west. The control of iron ores
was an important factor in the German seizure
of Lorraine in the war of 1870, and the subsequent
occupation of Lorraine, Alsace, and the Saar by
the French has had among its principal goals the
acquirement of mineral resources. The present
Italian unrest is due largely to the feeling that

Italy should have had some of the resources of North Africa as its part of the war spoils.

Germany's present deficiency in mineral supplies is perhaps the most striking case that could be cited. Here is a nation of great industrial development built up primarily around the coal of the Ruhr and the iron of Lorraine since 1870. Prior to the war it had been active in exploiting minerals in its colonies and elsewhere. Through the high development of its smelting enterprises, a heavy flow of minerals converged in Germany from all parts of the world. Now it has been stripped of its iron ores, of an important part of its coal, of its lead and zinc in Silesia, and of all the potential developments in its colonies. Even the remaining coal supply of the Ruhr was for a time endangered by the French occupation of the Ruhr. Germany has left only coal and potash. Outside sources of supply are now almost without exception controlled commercially and politically by former enemies. The situation is one of unstable equilibrium which will require wise and delicate handling if future trouble is to be avoided. The natural desire of the Germans to secure needed raw materials will be intensified by any restrictions or disadvantages placed by other powers on the flow of raw materials to Germany. On the other hand, these powers fear the German industrial development which will follow from unrestricted supplies. World efficiency and conservation will be retarded if the German contribution in the way of scientific organization is dispensed with. How will the problem be met?

Such conditions may not become the declared causes of war, but they furnish an atmosphere for the development of war psychology. Even though the minerals in question are normally available in adequate quantities during times of peace, there is always the fear that control would be in the hands of enemies in time of war.

There is nothing in sight to indicate that the force of these international rivalries for minerals will diminish in the near future. On the contrary, the increasing consumption of minerals and the growth of large commercial and political units of control, for the time being intensifies the contest. The problem of curbing these tendencies is a very difficult one without any obvious solution. Yet the situation contains some compensating elements, discussed under the subsequent heading, which promise some possibilities of amelioration.

Minerals as Deterrents to War

With the rapid concentration of commercial and political control there has come a narrowing of the fields of controversy, through greater intensity of rivalry in these fields. The Continental Steel Pact of Europe has eliminated some of the friction among European participants, but has intensified the competition with the iron and steel industries of the United States and Great Britain. The integration of the oil industry has tended to narrow competition to a few great units in a few important regions. Understandings between the Royal Dutch Shell (British) and Standard Oil (American) bid fair to eliminate additional zones of controversy in foreign fields. Thus far there is no change in the trend, and further consolidations and understandings, with consequent diminishing of the area of controversy, seem inevitable.

This line of reasoning might lead to the conclusion that if complete integration is accomplished, international competition for minerals will be eliminated as a potential cause of war. This Utopian view, however, is countered by the consideration that integration is yet far from complete and may never be so, and that in the meantime controversies, while diminished in number and area, are between more powerful contestants with greater forces at their disposal.

Also granting the likelihood of unit operation of many of the world's mineral industries, the problem remains as to what nations or groups of nations shall dominate them politically. The stronger nations will continue to compete for this position, unless they can find some satisfactory method of joint political control. The Franco-German iron and steel industry, based on the Ruhr coal and the Lorraine iron ore, seems likely to become commercially unified (see pages 62–63), but the struggle for political control may be a long one.[1]

During and since the World War the suggestion has come from various sources that nations controlling essential raw materials might prohibit their export to any country that breaks the peace (see pages 168–169). This might serve as a deterrent to nations without essential supplies or restrict the scale of war among such nations. It is difficult to see, however, how it could restrict the belligerent activities of nations controlling the supplies.

A retarding influence which in time may be considerable is the fact that no nation is really self-contained as to war supplies, and that with the vastly increasing demands of modern warfare, essential supplies in huge quantities must be obtained from all quarters of the globe, even by the nations most favored with domestic supplies. The problem of adequate preparation involves ways and means to keep these many channels open, which is probably beyond the power of the strongest nation. Realization of the appalling magnitude of the raw-material problem of preparedness may in time tend to delay hasty decisions to declare war.

[1] LEITH, C. K. "The World Iron and Steel Situation in Its Bearing on the French Occupation of the Ruhr," *Foreign Affairs*, vol. 1, pp. 136–151, 1923.

Chapter VIII

THE MINERAL FUTURE AND POLITICS

Present Trends

SALIENT trends in the mineral industry, as re-
viewed in preceding chapters, have been:

Large expansion of demand which could be satis-
fied only by concentration of production from a
comparatively few large reserves unequally distributed among the nations. Thousands of small operations have been relegated to the background as
factors of little importance.

The consequent interdependence of nations in
regard to minerals and a growing tendency toward
mineral specialization among the nations to an
extent which is making some of them the world
purveyors for certain minerals.

Growing necessity for consuming countries to look
abroad for essential supplies, and consequent increase in area and intensity of foreign exploitation.

Concentration of commercial control in a few
large companies, some of them international in
scope, which have acquired or are acquiring national
or world monopoly of some minerals. Such control

is peculiarly favored and invited by the dominance of the few large sources of supply which have been created by nature. For some minerals this tendency is just beginning to appear.

Dawning public recognition of this situation together with realization of the rôle of minerals in national security and economic welfare, their limited distribution, and their wasting and irreplaceable character.

As a natural consequence, increasing activity of governments in the conduct, control, and regulation of mineral industries, in the effort to prevent waste, to make each country as nearly as possible self-sustaining in regard to minerals, to prevent exploitation by alien interests, to secure needed minerals in other countries both for peace and for war. The more outstanding political measures to accomplish these purposes have been complete and partial nationalization of minerals in some countries, import tariffs and bounties and embargoes designed to develop local industries, special taxes based on the principle of wasting asset and heritage values, political aid to foreign exploitation, protection to foreign investments, restrictions against exploitation by aliens, direct financial aid and participation in mineral industries at home and abroad, conservation measures, closer regulation of industries as they approach the monopoly stage, encouragement of unification of the industry, in the interest of both efficiency and conservation, by commercial integration, cartels, and associations.

In general there has been a pronounced spread of government control of the mineral industry. As this is always done from national motives, the first result is a dismemberment of the world mineral industry, by creating more separate national units of industry than would exist if all the world's supplies and markets were open to all nations, and the best and most efficient world sources were used to the fullest extent. However, just as local commercial unification of the industry has often been followed by further integration with units of other countries, so in the political field, tightening control of national industries is here and there followed by international understandings. This is accomplished, not by the creation of any supernational government, but by a great variety of treaties and understandings regarding the open door and exploitation. International commercial combinations have far outstripped political understandings for their control, but such international political adjustments as have been made are all in the direction of conforming to the lead given by the commercial developments.

The Future

Looking to the future there seems to be little sign of early abatement of the political trends above sketched, but changes in emphasis appear almost inevitable.

Political Control of Minerals.—As commercial integration proceeds under the urge of efficiency and conservation, the problem of public control and regulation will become more acute. There is always the fear that if combination is allowed to go too far the situation will be exploited for private gain at the sacrifice of the public interest. Increasing size alone serves to focus public attention on outstanding units of the industry. The United States has been almost alone in a serious attempt to stop integration by legislation as a means of preserving competition and avoiding the consequences feared from private monopoly. At the same time commercial unification has been proceeding rapidly, has seemed to demonstrate its efficiency, and is being urged as a conservational measure in both the public and the private interest. The continuance of the present trend will almost certainly involve wider application of public regulation and control as a substitute for competition in insuring against excessive profits and wasteful exploitation.

Nor will the measures to be adopted be necessarily all restrictive. Overdevelopment and overproduction, with their train of commercial distress, bad labor conditions, and wastefulness, are becoming a too common condition for many raw materials, and there are indications that this may be a dominant question for many years to come. Already some affirmative steps of a political nature have been made to correct this condition, and these steps in effect are encouraging commercial unification (see pages 132–133).

As far as public control has yet been exercised it is mainly in the form of regulatory commissions of the type of the Interstate Commerce Commission and state utility, railway, or conservation commissions. This method preserves a wide field for private initiative and gain which are peculiarly required by the conditions of the mineral industry. Mining is a rapidly shifting, speculative, experimental field requiring the utmost variety of attack. Commercial integration can never go far enough to eliminate private initiative, even if it were desired. There are too many thousands of small mineral deposits and too much unexplored ground to be controlled by any commercial combination. No matter how ably manned, a bureaucracy could scarcely command a sufficient variety of talent, and even if this were possible, it would not be possible to secure public funds to explore all the remote and slightly promising leads now being followed by private interests. No official would dare to take such liberties in spending public funds.

It yet remains to be proved just what regulatory bodies and measures are best adapted to the problem, and whether, in fact, anything of this kind can be

[154]

worked out which will be really adequate. Already there is call from some quarters for nationalization of the energy resources, coal, oil, natural gas, and waterpower. The fact that nationalization is spreading in other countries will in itself tend to bring the problem up in the United States. This call can hardly be met successfully by blind opposition and insistence on complete freedom of commercial action. The best chance of avoiding it seems to be the intelligent development of the system already started, that is, concentration of commercial control under a kind of public supervision which will preserve private initiative and at the same time assure the public that the power thus conferred will be used in the public interest, and not exclusively for private gain.

Comparatively little has yet been done toward solving the problem of political control of world monopolies and of the larger units of the mineral industry of international scope. The fear of such large units, both in peace and in war, is already resulting in international discussion of their future control. Also the problem of world overproduction is to be met. The approach to these questions has thus far been mainly along national rather than international lines. In nearly all cases the driving power of these monopolies, commercial and political, is lodged in some one nation. As activities are projected beyond national boundaries, they are ad-

justed to meet the laws of other countries, but no one
country has political jurisdiction over all the activities. Where is the political control for the foreign
activities of the Copper Export Association, the
Sulphur Export Association, the Franco-German
potash combine, the Chilean nitrate producers, the
British tin industry, or several of the larger oil
companies? The question of political control of the
Continental Steel Pact of Europe, and of other
international cartels and associations, has already
proved a serious obstacle to their effective development. As long as such bodies function efficiently and
without discrimination among the nations there is
no urgent call for international control, but there
have been enough cases of inequitable and extortion-
ate use of these privileges to cause deep-seated fear
about their unrestricted activities for the future and
doubt whether an extension of purely national controls can ever solve the problem. The world is likely
to insist that these purveyors of essential commodities shall, in their foreign activities, come under some
sort of collective political control instead of reflecting
the political policies and ambitions of single nations.

Conservation.—Future legislation in the name of
conservation will involve much the same considerations as to how much can be left to private interest
and how much must be done by the state or government. There is general agreement that unification of
the industry is an essential step in conservation, that

the more important conservational measures are possible only under unified control, as has been proved by advances already made. Some conservationists believe that only direct government control can bring the desired results. Others believe that conservation would be achieved if the government would permit and encourage commercial unification. Conservation, like other phases of mineral development, requires an immense variety of initiative and attack. The conservational results so far obtained by private interests seem to warrant continuation of the method already started and deeply rooted in the industry, to see how far it can go, with the idea of introducing government control only as a supplement and aid in phases of the undertaking which time may prove to be beyond the power of private effort. However, long continuance of wasteful and chaotic conditions in the oil and coal industries may wear out the public patience and lead to some form of direct public control as a supposed solution of the problem.

Tariffs.—Mineral import tariffs will come in for extensive review and change. They are imposed by national self-interest in the effort to make the most of whatever mineral resources the nations have. In the post-war flare of nationalism it is but natural that these should go to unwarranted extremes for certain minerals and for certain nations. Such tariffs are hindering and more or less deflecting, but not stopping, the great international flows of minerals determined by geographic distribution. As the fact emerges that nations are really interdependent in regard to minerals on the new scale of requirements, the logical consequence will be a revision of tariffs to adjust the nations to this inescapable fact. There is opportunity in the United States, for instance, to review its surpluses and limitations in mineral supplies, to make provision for a permanent flow of the deficient minerals from foreign sources and to give intelligent aid to the disposal of its surpluses among other nations. Some of our tariffs are based on undue optimism concerning the mineral producing possibilities in our country. They cause only expense and irritation, and handicap national activities which are necessary abroad in the way both of acquiring and of disposing of minerals.

Protests against export tariffs, already voiced by many nations and international organizations, are likely to grow in volume. In some cases these tariffs are hastening the development of sources of supply in other parts of the world, and will have to be reduced for the sake of preserving volume of export, but if a mineral needed by the world is controlled by one or a few nations, and there is no other potential source, much international pressure is likely to be brought in the future on any nations which attempt to hold up the rest of the world by collecting an excessive tribute on essential raw materials.

THE MINERAL FUTURE AND POLITICS

The efforts of nations to build up local smelting, refining, and manufacturing industries by use of tariffs and taxes have often proved faulty in their perspective and have produced local results only at excessive cost.

In short, the future is likely to see a progressive adjustment of mineral tariffs to world conditions determined by highly unequal geographic distribution of mineral supplies. Much the same situation applies to bounties, embargoes, and various other measures used to supplement tariffs and substitute for them.

This is not a plea for unrestricted free trade. Experience has demonstrated the usefulness of protection in creating sound mineral industries, in preserving standards of living, and in yielding revenue. But experience has also shown that protective enactments cannot change the natural distribution of resources or create something out of nothing.

Taxation.—It remains to introduce some order and perspective into the chaos of mineral taxation. There are many inequalities in the treatment of various minerals by different local taxing bodies and further disparities in the levies by the state and Federal governments. The wasting-asset principle has been used as a basis for excessive local taxation in the United States, and at the same time it has been used by the Federal government to relieve

[159]

minerals of income taxes. Under the English income
tax law the principle of wasting assets is not
recognized. Throughout the field of taxation there
is evidence that the public regards minerals as
being in a special category of assets, but there is
confusion of thought as to the nature of this category. The taxation problem is closely involved
with practically all the other political problems
discussed in this chapter, and its solution on any
uniform and equitable basis will depend on the public policy adopted toward conservation, public control of minerals, tariffs, and international relations.

The Open Door.—The main objective for any
nation in regard to mineral supplies from abroad is
freedom to purchase the consumable product on a
price equality with all comers, including the citizens
of the country of origin, and non-discriminatory
conditions of transportation. Recognizing the right
of the country of origin to adopt reasonable safeguards against exploitation from without, and
wherever practicable to smelt and refine minerals
at home rather than to export them in crude form,
the consuming nations will insist on mutual equality
in regard to such opportunities as are granted for
exploitation from without. In case the country of
origin imposes unreasonable political conditions
which slow up necessary exploitation or result in
excessive costs of the consumable product, even
though these conditions are non-discriminatory,

the consuming country will bring political and commercial pressure to bear.

The consuming nations will also try to secure the widest latitude for their nationals in exploration and development of minerals in foreign countries and the privilege to export in crude form, for the sake of the profit to be derived and for the protection of extensive plant investments at home. This projection of effort into foreign fields is a natural consequence of the development of the necessary capital and skill in the industry. The job can seldom be done as efficiently by the country of origin, where past conditions have not developed equal capacity. Nevertheless, as desirable as these activities may be from the standpoint of the consuming country, insistence on them as rights can hardly go beyond the insurance of equal chances with other competing nations, unless the country of origin holds back essential supplies.

The open-door policy, therefore, relates to both rights and privileges. In the latter field it is subject to many limitations and must be highly elastic to meet the reasonable demands of countries of origin. Both rights and privileges are by their very nature reciprocal and require mutual adjustment of tariffs, taxes, and other political measures if an equitable result is to be reached. It has been altogether too common to rail at foreign countries for blocking our mineral activities abroad, or for undue exercise of monopoly controls, without stopping to consider how such questions are handled at home. The open-door policy in regard to minerals needs clarification and qualification before it can become established as an equitable basis for international dealing. It needs also coordination with policies relating to tariffs, taxes, and conservation.

The Gold Problem.—As one of many special problems that might be cited may be mentioned gold. Nearly the entire world is going over to the gold standard; the total demand for currency purposes is increasing faster than production; discoveries are not making up the deficiency; the arts alone are increasing their requirements to a point where they will soon absorb the annual new gold supply, if allowed to. The British Empire controls 70 per cent of the gold production of the world. Shall future production be left entirely to one political unit? Will reserves of gold ever become internationalized as a world yard-stick of values? What ratio shall be established between the demands of currency and the arts? Will special bounties and other artificial aids become necessary to augment the new gold supply, thereby lifting gold mining out of the category of purely commercial operations? What, in the meantime, is to be done with the increasing surplus of silver production, which is being displaced?

International Political Arrangements in Regard to Minerals.—So many of the outstanding mineral problems are international in scope, and national steps for their solution have thus far proved so inadequate, that in recent years there has been a flood of proposals for a more systematic international approach to the problem. At one extreme has been the proposal that minerals and other raw materials be administered by an international or supernational organization. The abdication of national control of raw materials to any such body is likely to be slow in coming. Minerals are almost the last of the national assets which the public would in any manner allow to be alienated. It is doubtful if the brains exist today which are adequate for such unit political control of minerals.

Most of the proposals aim at the development and modification of measures already employed in international dealings and the gradual consummation of political understandings adjusted to commercial necessity, to allow the maximum economic cooperation among the nations, without abdication of sovereign rights to a single international or supernational group. The nations which are weak in minerals, which now include Germany, foreseeing the possibility of the selfish administration of minerals by a few strong nations, are beginning to ask for international understandings and restrictions which will minimize this possibility. Similar steps are being urged in the interest of peace by many nations and organizations.

Out of the many and diverse suggestions that have been made, a few specific ones may be summarized to indicate various standpoints.

During the Armistice a suggestion came from British official sources that the exportable surplus of raw materials controlled by the Allies be allocated after the war by mutual agreement, substantially in continuance of the war procedure. The purpose was to make the Central Powers dependent on the Allies during the fulfillment of peace terms. Lists and estimates of key raw materials, including minerals, were drawn up and discussed at the Peace Conference. Nothing was done about it in drawing the Paris Treaty.

The French delegation to the Economic Commission of the Peace Conference submitted this proposal:

In order to put a stop as far as possible to the rivalries between people in the search for raw materials, to stamp out numerous causes of economic conflicts which are dangerous to the world's peace, and to do away with a natural unfairness arising from the fact that the riches of the world are unequally spread over its surface, the Allied and associate countries decide from now on that raw materials for industry will be entirely free of duty, both when entering and leaving a country. These raw materials are as follows: [Here follows a long list including most of the important minerals].

Sundry appeals for the consideration of the problem of raw materials were later presented to different international conferences. One of the first concrete proposals was offered at the International Miners' Congress held at Geneva in 1920. In a resolution the Congress expressed

the desire that there be constituted within a brief period an international office for the distribution of fuel, ores, and other raw materials indispensable for the revival of a normal economic life.[1]

The International Chamber of Commerce in 1921 passed a resolution reading as follows:

WHEREAS, every tax on export of raw materials must necessarily increase the cost of production and thereby hinder economic development and prevent economic restoration and

WHEREAS, it is desirable to put a stop to, as far as possible, rivalries between nations in their search for raw materials, to stamp out the cause of economic conflicts which may threaten peace, and to do away with the natural inequality arising from the fact that the riches of the world are un-equally spread over its surface, and to assure the rapid restoration of the world's commerce;

The Congress of the International Chamber of Commerce recommends:

The abolition of such export tax which Governments have imposed or may impose on the free movement of the raw materials which are included in the list attached hereto.

In the exceptional case of certain countries being obliged, in order to balance their budget, to maintain *provisionally* on these materials statistical or revenue duties imposed

[1] Etudes et documents, published by the Intern. Labor Office, Series A, No. 7, 1920.

upon exports, these duties should be applied without any discrimination whatever as regards countries. [Here follows a list containing most of the important minerals.][1]

In 1922 the Economic and Financial Committee of the League of Nations made a statement of general principles which should govern the attitude toward raw materials.

There is no question of challenging the incontestable right which states have to dispose freely of their natural resources, or of the output of their countries in respect of raw materials. It is legitimate that in exceptional circumstances they should be anxious to reserve them to themselves, and that they should have the power to subject them, at any time, to a régime in conformity with their natural economy. But it is not less incontestable that raw materials produced by one country being in many cases essential to the economic life of other states should not, unless in exceptional cases, be the object of restrictions or of differential regulations of such a nature as to injure the production of such states, or to impose upon them a systematic inferiority. It is undesirable particularly that measures of restriction taken by producing countries to meet exceptional situations should be so prolonged or altered as to change their character from being acts of precaution or defense to degenerate into measures of economic aggression.[2]

The World Economic Conference in 1927 passed a resolution and made recommendations regarding export taxes on raw materials:

[1] Resolution on Raw Materials passed at First Annual Meeting, Intern. Chamber of Commerce, London, June 27–July 1, 1921.

[2] Report on Certain Aspects of the Raw Materials Problem, League of Nations document, 1922.

THE MINERAL FUTURE AND POLITICS

The Conference is of the opinion that the free circulation of raw materials is one of the essential conditions for the healthy industrial and commercial ·development of the world.

It is therefore of the opinion that any export tax on raw materials or on the articles consumed by producers which has the effect of increasing the cost of production or the cost of living in foreign countries tends thereby to aggravate the natural inequalities arising from the geographical distribution of world wealth.

The Conference therefore considers that export duties should only be resorted to to meet the essential needs of revenue or some exceptional economic situation or to safeguard the vital interests of the country and that they should not discriminate between different foreign destinations.

The Conference therefore recommends:

1. That the exportation of raw materials should not be unduly burdened by export duties or any other taxes and that, even in cases where such duties or taxes are justified by fiscal needs or by exceptional or compelling circumstances, they should be as low as possible;

2. That, in any case, export duties on raw materials should never be imposed for the special purpose of subjecting foreign countries using such materials to an increased burden which will place them in a position of unfair inferiority as regards the production of the finished articles;

3. That export duties on raw materials, whether levied for revenue purposes or to meet exceptional or compelling circumstances, should never discriminate between different foreign destinations.[1]

[1] World Economic Conference Final Report, League of Nations document, p. 33, 1927.

In 1927 the Diplomatic Conference of the League of Nations drafted a convention (which was later ratified by the United States) for the abolition of import and export prohibitions and restrictions. The convention is not confined to raw materials, and it contains many specific exceptions of raw materials for different nations. It is about the first official multilateral recognition of principles of international control of raw materials.[1]

The British suggestion during the Armistice to continue the control of raw materials supplied to the Central Powers has recently been revived in modified forms. Sir Thomas Holland, in his presidential address to the British Association for the Advancement of Science, in 1929, proposed that

each country should add a simple rider to its Kellogg treaty with the United States, giving its government the power, if and when necessary, to prohibit the export of mineral products to any country that breaks the peace with any other member of the Pact. The very existence of any such power would be in itself sufficient automatically to enforce submission of the matters in dispute to the International Court of Justice.[2]

At the International Chamber of Commerce in 1930, Mr. E. N. Hurley, former chairman of the

[1] Questions économiques et financières, League of Nations document II, 71, 1927, and *ibid.*, II, 36, 1928. Published in final form in U. S. Treaty Series No. 811, Dept. of State, Washington, D. C., 1930.

[2] HOLLAND, SIR THOMAS H., International Movement of Mineral Products in Peace and War, *Jour. Roy. Soc. Arts*, vol. LXXVIII, No. 4030, p. 385, Feb. 14, 1930.

U. S. Shipping Board, pointed out that, as a means of abating war,

any modern nation could be paralyzed by the refusal of business organizations in the other countries to sell to it ten or twelve essential raw materials such as iron ore, rubber, manganese, nickel, aluminum, news-print pulp, copper, oils, tungsten, chromium, and mercury.[1]

It seems highly unlikely that such suggestions will be put into effect for a long time, but they raise interesting questions as to the possibilities of future control of minerals as a means of insuring peace.

Another approach to the problem is Briand's recent proposal for a political union of European states. He suggests that a political compact of this kind will clear the ground, through settlement of questions relating to national security, for economic pacts under the same union. Many such economic understandings have already been reached among these states, or are in the process of making as a result of economic pressure. Opinion is much divided as to whether political or economic organization shall precede, and as to the relative emphasis to be placed upon them. Certainly the removal of the fear of war should profoundly affect the nature of political control of minerals.

[1] HURLEY, E. N., Control of Strategic Raw Materials, *Army Ordnance*, p. 265, January–February, 1930.

Finally, beginning with the Paris Peace Conference, there have been various proposals to establish international fact-finding bodies, official and non-official, not only to assemble and coordinate the existing facts, but to develop principles and standards of fair practice. A small start in this field has been made by the League of Nations and by the World Economic Congress. So far as minerals are concerned, the information so far assembled is very fragmentary. Various national organizations have gone farther along this line (see Appendix A). Whether this work is done nationally or internationally, this seems to be a necessary first step for any approach to the problem.

Whatever form international measures may take, whatever our views of their desirability, further steps in this direction, both commercial and political, seem to be inherent in the impetus of movements already under way, which in turn seem to be direct consequences of nature's uneven apportionment of the principal mineral supplies among the nations.

To very large numbers of people the very word "international" is anathema. Any one discussing the problem is likely sooner or later to be called an "internationalist" with the implication that he is therefore not a good nationalist. This often rises from utter faith in the efficiency of nationalism in the solution of all problems, or from antagonism to specific international bodies such as the League of Nations or the World Court, which clouds the objective consideration of the international scope of economic forces.

It is difficult to secure public understanding of the fact that most of the questions outlined on these pages are by their very nature international in scope. Nearly all political policies and legislation touching them are yet narrowly national in their objectives. Their consequence to other nations is unknown or minimized. Enlightened self-interest alone requires an understanding of the broader situation. Satisfaction of our needs and wants is a world problem. The physical facts stand in the way of any nation reaching the stage of complete self-determination in regard to raw materials. The center of gravity for minerals will remain as before with the North Atlantic countries. Compromise and mutual concession are necessary if the world's resources are to be used in a way to afford anything approaching equal economic opportunity among the nations. It may be Utopian to expect that this condition will ever become the common goal of nations, but lessons from experience in the commercial field raise the hope that broader national self-interest may in the future come to be recognized as dependent on the welfare and security of all nations.

Appendix A

THE MINERAL INQUIRY

THE problems discussed in this book can yet be seen only in vague outline. Fact-finding agencies in this country and elsewhere have been busy during and since the war in assembling data, but these agencies have thus far been unable to keep up with the rapid changes in all parts of the world, and such results as have been obtained are very widely scattered and not available in satisfactory form for public use. In the United States, the Bureau of Mines, the Geological Survey, and the Department of Commerce have assembled much valuable information. The Committee on Foreign and Domestic Mining Policy of the Mining and Metallurgical Society of America has prepared useful surveys of several important minerals from a world standpoint. Its statement of general principles is quoted in Appendix B. A special report on manganese has been made by the Committee on Industrial Preparedness of the American Institute of Mining and Metallurgical Engineers for the War Department. Summaries for certain minerals have been prepared for trade publications and commercial organizations. Mineral specialists have published numerous articles on various phases of the situation. The subject has come up for discussion at the Williamstown Institute of Politics and in various other organizations interested in international affairs. Notable contributions have been made in many reports of the Imperial Mineral Resources Bureau of London.

Systematic studies of tariffs, concessions, treaties, and, in fact, nearly every political phase of the problem are yet very fragmentary.

The need of a more coordinated attack on the problem being apparent, a Mineral Inquiry has been inaugurated under the auspices of the American Institute of Mining and Metallurgical Engineers, which, by cooperative arrangements with other technical organizations, official bureaus, and several of the leading organizations devoted to the study of international affairs, will, it is hoped, focus much of the best available talent on the assembling, coordination, and interpretation of the pertinent facts, and make the information conveniently available to a wider public.

This inquiry is not an attempt to spread any particular view or propaganda, or to suggest any panacea. It is not known in advance what conclusions will be reached. It is a matter of self-education and of making sound data available in convenient form, with only such inferences and conclusions as seem to be unmistakably indicated by the facts.

The members of the central committee are: H. Foster Bain, G. Temple Bridgman, C. K. Leith, chairman, M. L. Requa, and J. E. Spurr.

Consulting members are: Jerome D. Greene of the Institute of Pacific Relations, Edwin F. Gay of the Social Science Research Council, Isaiah Bowman of the American Geographical Society, Nicholas Roosevelt of the Council on Foreign Relations, New York, and Thomas Walker Page of the Brookings Institution.

In Great Britain a committee has been appointed by the Empire Council of Mining and Metallurgical Institutions in cooperation with the Institution of Mining and Metallurgy, the Institution of Mining Engineers, and the Institution of Petroleum Technologists to further coordinate and consolidate the excellent work already started by the Imperial Mineral Resources Bureau and by the Empire Mining and Metallurgical Congress. Cooperative arrangements have been made between the American and British committees, which will be extended to professional bodies in other countries.

This book is in the nature of an opening statement of some of the problems which the Mineral Inquiry proposes to review, but it does not necessarily reflect the individual views of the members of the committee or attempt to anticipate conclusions which this committee may reach.

Appendix B

REPORTS OF THE COMMITTEE ON DOMESTIC
AND FOREIGN MINING POLICY OF THE
MINING AND METALLURGICAL
SOCIETY OF AMERICA

THE present Mineral Inquiry is in a sense an outcome of an earlier study by the Committee on Foreign and Domestic Mining Policy of the Mining and Metallurgical Society of America, begun in 1921. The reports of this committee and of its sub-committees on key minerals have been the basis of wide public discussion. It seems desirable, therefore, to quote in full the general statement of this committee[1].

A Report of the Committee on Domestic and Foreign Mining Policy of the Mining and Metallurgical Society of America, November, 1921

The subject assigned to this committee is one of interest to many nations of the world. It is within the domain of inter-

---

[1] In addition to the general reports here quoted special reports have been issued by sub-committees on antimony, chrome, graphite, manganese, mercury, petroleum, platinum metals, tin, tungsten, and vanadium. Additional reports are now in preparation.

national politics, and for this reason the members of the committee wish to emphasize the fact that they speak as individuals and not as representatives of any bodies with which they happen to be officially connected.

In the interest of efficient and conservational use of the world's mineral resources and in minimizing international difficulties arising from the discovery, development, transportation and marketing of mineral resources, the Committee on Domestic and Foreign Mining Policy of the Mining and Metallurgical Society of America offers a statement of elemental considerations which it believes should be basic to the formulation of laws and agreements affecting natural resources.

I. INTERNATIONAL MINERAL MOVEMENTS ARE NECESSARY CONSEQUENCES OF THEIR GEOGRAPHIC DISTRIBUTION

Mineral resources are wasting assets fixed geographically by nature, and change in this geographic distribution is not within our power. Some kinds of minerals are so widely distributed that nearly all countries have adequate supplies within their own boundaries or near at hand. Other minerals are so distributed that some parts of the world have a surplus and others a deficiency. No country is entirely self-sufficing in regard to either supplies or markets for all mineral commodities; in every country certain minerals are available in excess for export, while others are deficient and must be imported either in crude or manufactured forms. International exchange of minerals cannot be avoided if all parts of the world are to be supplied with needed materials.

The general nature and location of the fixed channels of international mineral exchange are not matters of conjecture; they are capable of reasonably definite statement.

APPENDIX

2. INTERNATIONAL MOVEMENTS OF CERTAIN MINERALS CANNOT BE STOPPED BY ENACTMENT

The necessary international movements of minerals may be aided or hindered by bonuses, preferential duties, tariffs, and embargoes. These measures may be locally and temporarily desirable for a great variety of reasons, but in general it is our belief that in the long run measures of this kind, aimed at the ultimate closing or diversion of the main international channels determined by nature, are doomed to failure, and that the effort to apply them will demand needless readjustment involving much unnecessary friction in international relations as well as in the orderly development of the mineral industry. When, for instance, it is proposed by tariff to foster an infant mineral industry, the geologic facts of the situation should be squarely faced to make sure that these controlling facts make such a course possible; otherwise there may be vast and useless expenditure of human energy in attempting to develop certain kinds of mineral resources in parts of the world where they are not present in sufficient abundance to be worthy of development. Mineral resources cannot be created by legislation.

Just as it is futile to attempt to make each state in the union self-supporting in regard to all minerals, so the effort to make each country independent of others is rendered impossible by the fact that nature has not distributed her resources in this fashion. Specialization of effort on particular minerals for particular localities seems essential to the conservation of human energy and to the most efficient utilization of nature's resources. To illustrate, if the distribution of raw materials is such that the United States can specialize on the production and export of copper, iron, and steel, and can do this with high efficiency, it seems hardly desirable that it should devote any large amount of effort to the development of its entirely inadequate tin and nickel supplies, which other parts of the world can produce more efficiently.

There are minerals which are so distributed that the necessity of international movement is not immediately apparent. For such minerals there may be reasons other than that of necessity for aiding or restricting this movement.

3. MINERALS SHOULD BE CONCENTRATED, SMELTED, OR FABRICATED NEAR SOURCE OF SUPPLY, WITH LIMITATIONS

In the interest of reduction of bulk and efficiency of transportation, the concentration, refining and fabrication of minerals near sources of supply should be encouraged wherever conditions permit. Countries fortunate enough to possess large supplies of a needed mineral, deficient elsewhere in the world, are entitled to the advantages that may come from conversion and fabrication of raw materials, unless local conditions make this possible only at excessive cost. Coal is the chief energy resource required for this work, and experience has shown that many minerals can be utilized with greater efficiency near sources of coal than near the sources of the minerals. With this consideration in mind, we do not favor the application of government measures of aid or restriction which attempt to establish a local smelting or fabricating industry where the supplies of raw materials, including coal, are such that the cost is excessive and efficiency low as compared with more favored localities.

We recognize as a qualifying factor the conditions of shipping which sometimes make it cheap and efficient to carry crude ores as a means of securing proper combination cargoes, and as a means of balancing local import and export requirements.

4. FREEDOM OF EXPLORATION IS ESSENTIAL

The exploration and development of mineral resources are continuously necessary to replenish ore reserves depleted by production. The present century has witnessed a greater consumption of mineral resources than has taken place in all previous history. Here in the United States the per capita consumption of minerals has multiplied ten times in only forty years. The problem of freedom of replenishment is not incidental, but of basic importance to the prosperity of the greatly magnified mineral industry which can be easily foreseen for the future. Any restrictions, national or international, which interfere with the necessary searching of the earth are in principle undesirable. We recognize the necessity and economic justification, during the early exploration stage and particularly in the case of petroleum, of rights covering large areas in order to induce and justify the expenditures necessary for careful exploration work in new regions. Where such concessions are safeguarded by the stipulation that within a limited period of, say, three to five years, the holder must select for retention a small percentage of the original exploration area, the result is development without exclusion. Exclusive concessions on large areas without such a reduction factor are economically unsound.

We believe that the aid and supervision of governments may be desirable in connection with exploration work, so far as they do not destroy the opportunity for private effort, but we further believe that government agencies cannot be substituted in this field for private initiative, except at the expense of that elasticity and variety of attack essential to the adequate solution of the complex problems of mineral development, and especially of mineral discovery.

In regard to this necessary activity of exploration we stand for equal opportunity and the open door—national and international. Equal opportunity and the open door are considered as implying, among other things, that, except under conditions of national crisis, there shall be no restriction on the issuance of mining licenses and concessions to foreigners or the transfer of concessions to foreigners; and that there be no restrictions on the nationality of the shareholders, managers, or directors in companies owning mining and exploration rights and concessions, allowing thereby the free purchase and acquisition by individuals of any nationality. The right of nations to control their own natural resources in times of war is of course paramount. There may be other special and local circumstances which might make such control desirable in times of peace. For the most part, however, all large mineral operations are by incorporated companies and the company being a creature of the state, the state may and usually does define very exactly its right and powers and in this way protects its own interest.

5. FREEDOM OF EXPLORATION IS TO BE PRESERVED IN BACKWARD COUNTRIES

Where backward countries possess important mineral supplies needed by the world we can see no escape from the conclusion, whatever the ethical merits of the case, that demand will make itself felt through political pressure of other countries. In such cases we favor joint action by governments to secure equal opportunities for all nationals. If circumstances require that pressure be brought by one government the end to be sought should be the opening up of the territory not only to the government bringing the pressure for its exclusive benefit, but to all nationals. Disregard of this principle has been the cause of much international friction.

APPENDIX

In view of recent discoveries, borax should probably be added to the list.

So far as the available quantity is concerned there is no reason why these minerals should not be exported. Prosperity of the industry may depend largely on maintaining foreign outlets, in which case these should not be closed by restrictions requiring local conversion and fabrication where this means excessive cost, or by import taxes inviting retaliation on minerals of which our own supply is deficient. For instance, export of coal from the United States is a natural consequence of our large supplies, the needs of other countries, and our ability to produce more efficiently and cheaply than certain other coal-exporting nations. We are in a position to do the world an efficient service. We also help ourselves by supplying an equalizing and stabilizing factor to an industry handicapped by such seasonal demand that the average coal mine is idle over a third of the year. We more fully utilize our capacity for production. Without increase of imports there is little room for further development of coal export trade without unbalancing the ratio between imports and exports.

B. The United States has certain minerals of adequate supply but without great excess or deficiency. The supplies of many important minerals in the United States approximately balance domestic requirements without considerable exportable surplus. Small amounts of these minerals have been and will continue to be imported and exported because of special grades or backhaul, or because of cheaper sources of foreign supply. Such imports are not, however, for the most part, essential as a source of supply. This list includes aluminum and bauxite, arsenic, artificial abrasives and emery (except Naxos emery), asphalt and bitumen, barite, bismuth, bromine, building stone (except Italian marble), common stone, sand and gravel, cadmium, feldspar, fluor-

[183]

spar, fuller's earth, gold, gypsum, lead, lime, magnesite, mineral paints (except umber, sienna, and ocher from France and Spain), molybdenum, oil, pyrite, salt (except special classes), talc, titanium, tripoli and diatomaceous earth, and zinc.

For minerals of this group, the domestic supplies are such that they do not constitute compelling reasons for opening or closing channels of international movement. There may or may not be other reasons, but it is our purpose here only to indicate the effect of known supplies on the question of international movements of minerals.

The inclusion of oil among the minerals of class B, in which the country is approximately self-supporting, requires some explanation and qualification. The United States leads the world in its oil production, but it also leads the world in consumption. If our exportation of refined products were eliminated we could probably get along for some time on the domestic production. As it is, imports from other countries, particularly Mexico, have been necessary in recent years to balance the export of refined products. The industry is on such an efficient basis that the United States is able to perform a service to the rest of the world in gathering and distributing this material. It seems desirable, in the interest of our continued service to the world, that channels of import and export be kept open. Looking forward to the future, we are doubtful whether the domestic production will long keep up with domestic demand; this consideration is an additional reason why channels of import should be maintained.

In the exploration and development of oil, American initiative and capital have proved most efficient and should be allowed the fullest latitude both at home and abroad, with the purpose of insuring adequate supplies for future home consumption and supplies for refinement and export to the rest of the world. The Government can aid in securing and preserving this opportunity.

Self-interest plays so large a part in asking these opportunities for ourselves that we deplore criticism of other countries for asking the same for themselves, so far as their resulting activities do not impair a fair field for private initiative and competition.

C. Certain minerals exist in the United States in inadequate amounts. The United States will be dependent on foreign sources for a considerable fraction of its supply of antimony, asbestos, ball clay, kaolin, chalk, chromite, corundum, garnet, certain grades of graphite, grinding pebbles, manganese, mercury, mica, monazite, Naxos emery, nitrates, potash, precious stones, pumice, tungsten, vanadium and zirconium.

D. The United States lacks certain minerals almost entirely. The United States will in the future, as in the past, depend on other countries almost entirely for its nickel, cobalt, platinum, tin, gem diamonds, black diamonds, or "carbonado," and diamond dust and bort.

Import of minerals of classes C and D will continue to be necessary and can be stopped only at great cost. Future exploration may disclose adequate supplies of some of those minerals in which the United States is now deficient but for the most part we believe that the geologic conditions are sufficiently well known to make this outcome unlikely. With certain exceptions noted below, we believe that any attempt by legislation to keep foreign supplies out and to make domestic supplies of these minerals suffice for United States needs will not succeed except at excessive cost in efficiency and money. Such a course also would mean depletion of limited supplies which may seriously endanger the country in a time of critical future need. In the meantime, governmental restrictions on imports (probably inducing retaliatory measures abroad) are likely to make it more difficult for American enterprise to find and develop needed resources of these minerals in foreign countries where the geologic conditions are more favorable.

Conditions under which import taxes on minerals of classes C and D might be desirable. As long as import channels of these minerals are not closed we do not oppose tariffs or other measures which are designed to offset differences in living costs and to aid in maintaining a sound nucleus for an industry which might be useful in crises. We believe, however, that such measures have practically very limited application in view of the physical facts of the situation.

Luxuries such as diamonds and platinum used for jewelry may well afford to pay import taxes.

We would favor protection on domestic minerals known to exist in large quantities and capable of efficient utilization, but handicapped in their competition with foreign supplies by trade and technical customs. In these cases there should be careful consideration of possibilities of adapting our extensive low-grade reserves to our needs, with a view of finding whether feasible and efficient processes for their use may not be developed without excessive cost. If so, some measure of protection would be reasonable. For instance, there are very extensive deposits of flake graphite in the United States, many of which are handicapped by a fineness of texture which is said to make them undesirable for one of their principal uses, the manufacture of crucibles. War experience indicated that the American grades could be used to a larger extent than had before been anticipated; but with the resumption of peace conditions, foreign supplies have again dominated the market. Without committing ourselves definitely for or against a tariff, we suggest that a case of this kind affords a reasonable field for investigation as to the possible application of a tariff.

APPENDIX

CONCLUSION

This statement of principle emphasizes nature's distribution of minerals as a basic factor in determining the international movements of minerals. It does not attempt to cover all the qualifying economic factors in the situation.

These considerations are presented from the point of view primarily of the broad self-interest of the mineral industry of the United States, but they are also vital to the preservation of friendly international relations. We are confident that a common understanding of these elementary facts of geographic distribution of minerals, and of the consequent necessary mineral movements determined by nature, is an important first step in minimizing international difficulties.

The interests and ambitions of the different parts of the mineral industry in foreign matters are so extremely diverse, and each of them is urged so vigorously that it is difficult to discern what, if any, are the underlying aims and principles of the industry as a whole. The industry itself is presumably better qualified to speak on these matters than others, and yet to the public its representations must sound like a babel of special interests. This is perhaps an inevitable consequence of the scattered geographic development of the mineral industry, but the industry has now reached such large proportions and so often overlaps national boundaries that the formulation of a unit policy is of vital national concern.

Respectfully submitted,

C. K. LEITH, *Chairman*, Professor of Geology, University of Wisconsin.

H. FOSTER BAIN, Director, U. S. Bureau of Mines.

S. H. BALL, Mining Geologist, New York.

[187]

WORLD MINERALS AND WORLD POLITICS

VAN. H. MANNING, Director, Technical Research, American Petroleum Institute, New York.
GEORGE OTIS SMITH, Director, U. S. Geological Survey.
A. C. VEATCH, Consulting Geologist, New York.
H. V. WINCHELL,[1] Mining Geologist, Los Angeles.
POPE YEATMAN, Mining Engineer, New York.

Progress Report of the Committee on Foreign and Domestic Mining Policy, June, 1925

The general committee herewith notes some of the salient features of the discussion to date of the general principles presented in its report of November, 1921.

1. *International mineral movements are necessary consequences of their geographic distribution.* There has been no dissent from this statement. On the contrary, many specific illustrations have been offered to demonstrate this conclusion. It should, however, always be borne in mind that the international movements at any given moment are dependent on the geographical distribution of the *developed* deposits and the character of the development in each case, and not on the total world reserves or the location of such reserves.

2. *International movements of certain minerals cannot be stopped by enactment.* One qualification has been suggested —that legislation sometimes permits the development of an industry where it has not existed before, and in this way changes international movements. This qualification divides itself into two parts: (*a*) The creation of an industry by means of preferential duties or bonuses, which is an aspect of the subject that was discussed in the original statement, and (*b*) the development which is made possible by the changing of laws relating to mining, where such changes remove conditions and requirements that are commercially

[1] Deceased.

not suited to the region involved, and substituting therefor terms and conditions which justify the investment of the capital necessary for the development of the deposits therein.

The participation exacted by a government—which is only one of the factors concerned in the relation between mining laws and regulations and successful development— may be fixed at so high a rate as to prevent the commercial development of a given deposit, and in such cases the lowering of the government participation to a point which will leave an attractive margin of profit for the operating company, would result in the creation of a new industry in the country involved.

3. *Minerals should be concentrated, smelted, or fabricated near source of supply, with limitations.* Attention is called to the fact that the present practice is to concentrate minerals near the source of supply, because of high transportation costs of unconcentrated ore, but that smelting and fabricating frequently can be done to better advantage near industrial centers than near sources. Two partially opposing tendencies are noted: (*a*) Increase of local legislation to require smelting or fabrication near sources of supply, even though this be at higher cost; (*b*) the carrying of concentrated materials greater distances to industrial centers, because of the increasing financial power and requirements of these centers. The committee in general favors the localization of these operations where they can be most efficiently and cheaply carried on, but recognizes the fact that national interests may in some cases warrant localization near sources of supply, where this can be done without too excessive cost.

4. *Freedom of exploration is essential.* The discussion of this principle reflects the growing recognition of the limita-

tion of even the largest mineral reserves and the necessity for far-flung exploration, as little hampered as possible by purely national or local considerations.

5. *Freedom of exploration is to be preserved in backward countries.* The fact is noted that, on the whole, mineral reserves have been more intensively explored and developed near the great industrial centers of the world than farther afield, and that more of the future discoveries must be made in outlying countries, which are commercially less developed and which are not in a position to do this work effectively for themselves. Political and commercial pressure on these countries therefore seems inevitable. On the other hand, the present tendency of legislation the world over seems to be in the direction of restricting opportunities for exploration by extra-national interests.

6. *Government co-operation is desirable in securing the open door to mineral exploration and development.* This principle is warmly endorsed, particularly in the report of the petroleum committee, and specific suggestions are made as to the manner in which the government may co-operate. There is widespread feeling that the attitude of our government has not yet reflected the existence of any unified and persistent policy in regard to minerals. The open door is the historic policy of this government, but in regard to mineral development there are opportunities for specific application of this policy that the committee feels can properly be urged.

7. *The mineral reserves of the United States in their world relations.* In our first report an attempt was made to classify the minerals possessed and needed by the United States under the following sub-headings: (A) Minerals available in large quantities for export; (B) minerals of adequate supply but without excess or deficiency; (C) minerals in inadequate amounts; (D) those almost entirely

lacking. As was anticipated, this attempt to be specific has presented a good target for criticism, but on the whole the classification has stood the test. Gold, now put in Class B, is thought by some to belong in Class A, and by others to belong in Class C, because of the deficit caused by demand for the arts. It is suggested that helium should be included in Class A as a mineral of which the United States has almost exclusive control. The principal criticism comes in regard to the minerals named in Class C, supposed to be in inadequate amount. Ball clay, kaolin, corundum, garnet, and certain grades of graphite are thought by some people to belong in Class B. Others would add chromite, mercury, tungsten, and manganese to the list to be transferred to Class B. As for the Class D minerals, which seem to be lacking almost entirely in the United States, question is raised about cobalt; though small in quantity, it is thought by some to be adequate for our purposes.

A second group of comments on the classification of minerals calls for additional subdivision. For instance, between Class B and Class D a subdivision of minerals of doubtful supply and high cost, which might be developed by an experimental tariff, and another group of minerals, the quantity of which is known to be adequate, but which are retarded by high costs. Another suggestion is that the Group B minerals be subdivided into (1) minerals with exportable surplus if the rest of the world were not so well supplied and (2) those of which we can produce enough for ourselves only when cheaper imports are not available.

Some of these suggestions are based on extensive knowledge and an impartial attitude; others come from parties personally interested in the exploitation of one or another mineral, who are anxious to secure protection to allow exploration and development. Many of the supporting arguments and data had already been considered in formulating the original classification, and the committee will postpone any attempt to revise its list until special reports have been received from most of the minerals mentioned. There is of course much difficulty in making any general classification which is sufficiently comprehensive, elastic, and at the same time specific, to cover all minerals. One of the outstanding difficulties is the variation of amounts of ore available with fluctuating prices. With high prices it may be possible to produce profitably an ore of inferior grade and ship it long distances, while, at low prices, it cannot be mined in competition with foreign ore. The *available* reserve therefore varies in time and place. The classes named by the committee are so broadly defined that the statement of quantity will hold under a wide variety of prices, but under exceptional conditions of extremely high or extremely low prices, certain of the minerals named would need to be transferred to other classes.

Tariff. In some quarters the report of the general committee was interpreted as a free-trade document. For some of the minerals named the facts of reserve supply taken by themselves favor free-trade; for others, some measure of protection. The committee expressly disclaims any intention of discussing tariffs *per se*, including the many economic and political questions which must be taken into account in addition to the facts of supply. Nevertheless the committee believes that such facts should not be ignored in framing tariffs. In the special reports of the sub-committees belief is repeatedly expressed that even if a tariff might be temporarily helpful to certain minerals existing in inadequate amount and off grades, it will also cause dangerous depletion of reserves vital to national security in times of war, when the United States might be cut off from foreign

APPENDIX

sources. In view of the ever-growing size of the drafts on
our domestic mineral reserves, and of the better understanding of the limits of many of these reserves, we believe that
a wise national policy should in general favor the free use
of foreign sources of supply of minerals which we do not
have in adequate quantities, in order to conserve our own
resources; that if we long continue on our present policy of
exploiting our resources to the utmost, regardless of their
limitations, some of them will be soon exhausted, making
the United States entirely dependent upon other countries
for these minerals in times of peace, and dangerously dependent in times of war. Also it has been suggested that a
"tariff in kind" might well be assessed on minerals for the
purpose of accumulating a war reserve. This question is now
under study.

Respectfully submitted,
C. K. LEITH, *Chairman*,
H. FOSTER BAIN,
S. H. BALL,
VAN. H. MANNING,
GEORGE OTIS SMITH,
A. C. VEATCH,
POPE YEATMAN.

INDEX

A

Africa, 67
  capital control, 68
  copper, 40
  exploitation, 68
  iron ore, 67
  manganese ore, 10
  petroleum, 36, 67
  political control, 68
Ajo, Ariz., copper, 26
Alabama, iron ore, 7
  tax, 84
Alaska, copper, 10
  placer deposits, 23
Alberta, coal, 37, 52
Algeria, minerals, 67
Allies, raw materials, 139, 164, 168
Alsace, mineral resources, 11, 42, 60, 145
Aluminium Ltd., bauxite, 42
Aluminum, British Guiana, 52
  from clay, 33
  control, 14
  Dutch Guiana, 52
  Europe, 52
  Germany, 92, 142
  Great Britain, 56
  Italy, 64
  substitution, 33
  technology, 29
  United States, 48
Aluminum Company, bauxite, 42

American Institute of Mining and
  Metallurgical Engineers, 77
Andean region, copper, 39
  (*See also* Chile and Peru.)
Anglo-Persian Oil Company, 87, 110
Anshan, Manchuria, iron ore, 99
Anti-trust laws, 82, 133, 134, 136
Antimony, China, 70
  Czechoslovakia, 66
  France, 60
  Germany, 61, 62
  Great Britain, 56, 57
  Mexico, 54
  United States, 49
Appalachians, natural gas, 37
  petroleum, 24
Argentina, agreement with United
  States, 85
  government participation, 96
  lease contracts, 95
  petroleum, 55, 96, 97, 98, 111
Arizona, copper, 10, 26
Arkansas, severance taxes, 109
Arsenic, Mexico, 54
  United States, 48
Asbestos, Canada, 51, 52, 106
  control, 14
  France, 60
  Germany, 61, 62, 142
  Great Britain, 56
  Russia, 66
  South Africa, 52, 68
  United States, 50

INDEX

INDEX

INDEX

France, mining law, 111
  North Africa, 91, 117
  political control, 98
  preferential duties, 91
  Société Minerais et Metaux, 91
  subsidies, 91
Franco-German, iron and steel, 148, 149
  potash, 82, 83, 101, 122, 156
Fuel, International Miners' Congress, 165
  production, 3
  (*See also* Coal, Petroleum, and Natural gas.)
Furness, J. W., and Jones, L. M., 72
Fushun, Manchuria, coal, 99

G

Gay, Edwin F., 174
Geographic changes in mineral production, 30
Georgia, manganese ore, 10
Germany, 61, 91
  activity since the World War, 62
  agreements with France and Poland, 63, 92
    with United States, 85
  brass, 142
  cartels, 92
  conservation, 138
  Great War, 145
  iron and steel production, 62
  minerals, 8, 11, 12, 17, 23, 37, 61–63, 91, 92, 111, 113, 142, 144, 145, 146, 163
  rehabilitation since World War, 63
  Silesia, 66

Gold, 4, 10, 43, 44, 125
  Australia, 23, 43, 68
  British Empire, 57, 162
  Canada, 26, 43, 52
  China, 70
  Comstock, 23
  control by British interests, 17
  Cripple Creek, Colo., 23
  East Indies, 70
  Goldfield, Nev., 23, 26
  India, 70
  Japan, 70
  Kirkland Lake, Ont., 26, 43
  Korea, 70
  Leadville, Colo., 23
  Mexico, 54
  North America, 43
  Porcupine, Ont., 26, 43
  problem, 162
  production, 25, 26
  Rand, 43
  Russia, 66
  South Africa, 67
  Tonopah, Nev., 23, 26
  United States, 23, 26, 43
Gold Coast, manganese, 10, 67, 88
Goldfield, Nev., 23, 26
Graphite, 43
  Ceylon, 43
  Czechoslovakia, 66
  France, 60
  Germany, 61, 142
  Great Britain, 56
  Italy, 64
  Madagascar, 43, 60, 67, 68, 106
  Mexico, 54
  Russia, 66
  Spain, 64
  United States, 50

INDEX

Interstate Commerce Commission, 154
Ioannou, Florence K., 106
Iraq Petroleum Company, Mesopotamia, 118, 132
Iron alloys, 33
Iron ore, 38
  Africa, 67
  Algeria, 67
  Anshan, Manchuria, 99
  Australia, 38, 68, 69, 71
  Belgium, 63
  Brazil, 28, 38, 51, 55, 97
  Canada, 52, 89
  Chile, 51, 55, 71
  China, 71, 99, 122
  control, 14, 15, 88
  Cuba, 38, 51
  Czechoslovakia, 66
  distribution, 7–8
  Dutch East Indies, 39, 71
  European, imports, 38
  Far East, 39
  Formosa, 99
  France, 60, 61
  Germany, 61, 62, 146
  Great Britain, 23, 38, 57, 88
  India, 28, 38, 39, 71
  industrial power, 142
  international movement of, 13
  Italy, 64
  Japan, 70, 71
  Korea, 71
  Lake Superior region, 24, 26, 38, 39, 84
  Lorraine, 60, 63, 139, 145, 146, 149
  Malay, 71, 99
  Manchuria, 70, 71, 111
  Mexico, 54
  Minnesota, 82, 108, 109, 134

Iron ore, Morocco, 64, 67, 145
  Newfoundland, 38
  North Africa, 61
  Norway, 65
  Pacific Basin, 39
  Philippines, 39, 71
  Poland, 65
  in pre-Cambrian rocks, 27–28
  production, 4, 44
  Russia, 38, 66, 93
  Spain, 23, 38, 64, 66
  Sweden, 65, 66
  technology, 29
  Tunisia, 67
  Union of South Africa, 28, 38, 67, 88
  United States, 26, 28, 38, 39, 48, 50
  Venezuela, 55
Iron and steel, France, 62, 148, 149
  Germany, 62, 148, 149
  Great Britain, 148
  India, 72
  industrial power, 142
  Japan, 99
  New South Wales, 68
  Poland, 65
  production, 3, 8
  Saar, 62
  Union of South Africa, 88
  United States, 8, 48, 148
Italy, 64, 94
  concessions, 94
  conservation, 94
  exploration in North Africa, 64
  minerals, 17, 18, 41, 64, 94
  national defense, 94
  North African resources, 145, 146

[203]

Italy, oil stocks, 141
  steel syndicate, 94

J

Japan, 98, 99
  Asia, 99
  Australian iron ore, 69, 71
  China, relations with, 99
  closed door, 116
  foreign policy, 99
  government participation, 98, 99
  Hanyehping Iron and Coal Company, 99
  industrial development, 72
  iron and steel, 99, 111
  Manchuria, activities in, 99, 111
  minerals, 70, 99, 111
  mining rights, 98, 116
Japanese-Chinese, Yangste iron, 122
Jones, L. M., and Furness, J. W., 72

K

Kansas, natural gas, 37
Kellogg Treaty, United States, 168
Keweenaw, Mich., copper, 24
Key minerals, 140, 141, 142, 144, 145
Kirkland Lake, Ont., gold, 26, 43
Kiruna district, Sweden, iron ores, 7
Korea, 70, 71, 98

L

Lake Superior region, copper, 39
  iron ore, 7, 24, 26, 38, 39, 84
Land grants, railway, 82

Latin-America, concessions, 95
Latin-American countries, 94
  mineral ownership, 95, 114
  political control, 94, 97
Latvia, agreement with United States, 85
Lead, 41
  Algeria, 67
  Australia, 41, 68
  Burma, 41, 70
  Canada, 41, 52
  Coeur d'Alene district, 26
  control, 14
  Europe, 23, 41
  France, 60, 91
  Germany, 61, 62
  Great Britain, 23, 56
  industrial power, 142
  Italy, 64, 94
  Mexico, 41, 54
  North Africa, 61
  Peru, 55
  Poland, 65
  Russia, 66, 93
  Silesia, 146
  sources, 11
  Spain, 23, 64, 106
  Sullivan Mine, B. C., 41
  Sweden, 65
  United States, 11, 26, 41, 48, 50
Leadville, Colo., 23
League of Nations, 86, 105, 122, 168, 170, 171
Lease contracts, South America, 95
Leasing Act, United States, 81, 85, 86, 98, 114, 117, 136
Leith, C. K., 54, 69, 77, 125, 149, 174
Lignite, Germany, 38
Limestone, 15-16

INDEX

INDEX

INDEX

INDEX

Utah, copper, 10
zinc, 40

V

Vanadium, 41
control, 14
Peru, 51, 55, 106
source, 10
United States, 51
Venezuela, agreement with
United States, 85, 98
exploitation, 133
lease contracts, 95
minerals, 9, 35, 51, 55, 97
Vertical trust, control by, 15

W

Wakefield, Roberta P., 106
Wales, coal production, 9
Wallace, Benjamin B., 77
War, raw materials, 108, 140, 141, 149
War Department, United States, 172
Water power, United States, 4, 5, 31, 48–49
Webb Export Trade Act, United States, 85, 112
West Virginia, petroleum, 35
Western Europe, shifts in iron and steel industry, 62
Williamstown Institute of Politics, 173
Wilson Tariff Act, United States, 113
World Court, 171
World Economic Conference, 122, 166, 167, 170

Z

Zinc, 40
Algeria, 67
Australia, 41, 68
Bawdwin district, Burma, 41
Belgium, 63
Broken Hill district, Australia, 41, 62
Burma, 41, 70
Canada, 40, 41, 51, 52
control, 14, 15, 16
electrolytic smelting, 40
Europe, 40, 41
France, 60, 91
Germany, 61, 62, 63
Great Britain, 56
Idaho, 40
industrial power, 142
Italy, 41, 64, 94
Manitoba, 40
Mexico, 40, 41, 51, 54
Montana, 40
New Jersey, 40
Newfoundland, 40, 51
North Africa, 61
Peru, 51
Poland, 51, 63, 65
production, 4
Quebec, 40
Russia, 66, 93
South America, 41
Spain, 41, 64
Sudbury district, Ontario, 40
Sullivan Mine, B. C., 40
Sweden, 65
Tennessee, 40
Tri-state district, 24, 40
United States, 11, 40, 41, 48, 49
Utah, 40
Zirconium, 41

[213]